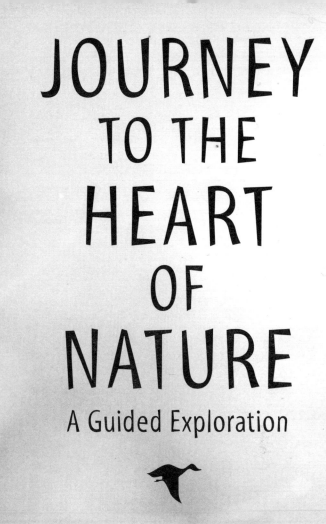

JOURNEY
TO THE
HEART
OF
NATURE

A Guided Exploration

by JOSEPH CORNELL
and MICHAEL DERANJA

DAWN PUBLICATIONS

DEDICATION

"Keep close to nature's heart."

–John Muir

The publisher and author disclaim any liability for injury that may result from following the techniques and instructions described in this book, which could be dangerous in certain situations.

ISBN 1-883220-06-8

Published by DAWN Publications
14618 Tyler Foote Road
Nevada City, California 95959
916-292-3482

Printed on recycled paper using soy based ink

10 9 8 7 6 5 4 3 2 1
First Edition

FOREWORD

The publication of *Journey to the Heart of Nature* marks a significant milestone for World Scouting.

The Scout Movement has, since its inception, helped and encouraged its members to care for the environment. Today, more than 16 million Scouts, boys and girls, in over 150 countries around the world, are committed to helping to make the world a better place in which to live.

When young people join the Scout Movement, they make a Promise to do their duty to God, to others and to themselves. Scouts are challenged to reflect these principles in all that they do. Thus, in their discovery of Nature and their actions in favor of the environment, Scouts see a spiritual and a social dimension as well as opportunities to develop themselves physically and intellectually. The Founder of the Scout Movement, Robert Baden-Powell, described the essence of this approach to the education of young people when he wrote: *"For those who have eyes to see and ears to hear, the forest is at once a laboratory, a club and a temple."*

It is in this context that World Scouting invited Joseph Cornell to write this book, for use principally by Scouts around the world.

Joseph's unique experiential approach to environmental education, so effectively conveyed in his earlier works such as *Sharing Nature with Children* and *Sharing the Joy of Nature*, fits perfectly with "the Scout method," including its emphasis on learning by doing and contact with Nature. Joseph has extensive experience working with Scouts and Scout leaders and has recently participated in two international seminars organized by World Scouting as part of a current effort to raise the profile of environmental education and action in the Movement.

World Scouting is grateful to Joseph Cornell and to Dawn Publications for making *Journey to the Heart of Nature* available as a new resource for use by Scouts—and, of course, by the many others, young and perhaps not-so-young, who will find in it inspiration for their own exploration of the wonders of the natural world.

Jacques Moreillon
Secretary General
World Organization of the Scout Movement

CONTENTS

*J*ourney to the Heart of Nature was written as a guided exploration for young adults (ages 12-17); but older children (ages 9-11), and adults as well, will enjoy its stories and activities. In fact, many adults will want to use this book for their own personal inspiration.

The *Journey to the Heart of Nature* reader chooses and explores a special place in nature. During a series of five visits, stories and activities help the reader discover the area's uniqueness and beauty.

Direct contact with trees, birds, and summer meadows awakens a natural wonder and curiosity. As John Burroughs wrote:

"Turn them loose in the country...bathe the spirit in natural influences.... It is time enough to answer children's questions when they are interested enough to ask them. Knowledge without love does not stick; but if love comes first, knowledge is pretty sure to follow."

Too much emphasis on facts, before genuine interest has been aroused, generally does more harm than good. Personal discovery, carefree play, and use of the physical senses is a far more effective approach to awakening an interest in nature. Learning to love and care for nature in one place will encourage a love for all of nature.

Most important, love for nature is the fertile soil in which environmental concern can take root and grow. Sigurd Olson, the American wilderness guide, said, "Without love for the land, conservation lacks meaning or purpose, for only in a deep and inherent feeling for the land can there be dedication to preserving it...."

Although this book is written as if a young person is doing the activities alone, many adults will want to go along and share these nature experiences with their young friends. You'll find that in this way *Journey to the Heart of Nature* creates a unique bonding experience. All young readers are asked to choose an adult to supervise their visits and share their discoveries. While working with teenagers, the adult's role may be as simple as introducing the program and reviewing plans for visits to the site to ensure safety. With children (ages 9-11), the leader will want to become a co-participator, reading the text, helping with the activities, and recording their thoughts on paper.

Safety is an important consideration. In determining whether unsupervised activity is appropriate, carefully consider such factors as level of maturity, outdoor experience, the physical terrain, and the presence of people in the area.

The book can be used in a variety of ways. If a natural area is unavailable, much of the material can be adapted for use in open countryside, a city park, or any place direct interaction with nature is possible. The activities and stories can also be readily used with groups. Schools, Scout groups, and environmental organizations have successfully used many of these activities for years. The Leader's Guide on page 112 gives detailed suggestions for adapting the program for different situations.

Adult leaders should first familiarize themselves with each of the visits and activities, paying special attention to "Finding Your Special Place," on page 16, and "Getting Ready for the Night" on page 88, as well as the Leader's Guide. A fine way to introduce the activities is to read the first pages of Visit One aloud.

Good luck! I wish you many rewarding experiences on your *Journey to the Heart of Nature.*

Joseph Cornell
Nevada City, California
February, 1994

Guidelines

FOR A SUCCESSFUL
JOURNEY

1

First Visit

Choosing & Exploring Your Area

"Walk away quietly in any direction and taste the freedom of the mountaineer.... Climb the mountains and get their good tidings. Nature's peace will flow into you as sunshine flows into trees. The winds will blow their own freshness into you, and the storms their energy, while cares will drop off like autumn leaves."

–John Muir, American naturalist and conservationist

There's a treasure I'd like to share with you, one that is hidden at the heart of nature. To find it, you'll need a special place outdoors where you can be alone and feel free; a place where you can see animals, hear a bird's song, and feel the wind. Perhaps you already know of such a place. If not, you'll have a chance later on as you read this book to discover one. As you explore your area, you'll have many adventures, like the ones I had when my own journey began...

When I was a young boy growing up in northern California, I had a special place. I was seven years old when I discovered it, still much too young to go there by myself. Fortunately, one day the animals from my special place came and visited me instead.

I was playing alone on a cold, foggy morning when I heard a startling series of "whouks!" approaching through the air. I peered intently through the thick fog, hoping to catch a glimpse of the mystery birds that were making the sound.

Seconds passed and the bird cries got louder. They were approaching in a direction that would take them right over my head! I could hear their wings slapping close above, when all of a sudden a big flock of pearl-white Snow Geese burst through the fog. It was almost as if the sky had created them. For five or six wonderful seconds I could see their sleek and graceful forms—then they disappeared in the fog again. Their fading calls seemed to be saying "Follow us! Follow us!"

Some years later, when I was old enough to follow my bird visitors, I discovered that they lived in the nearby marshes and grain fields. Over the years, I had many chances to go out and observe them.

I remember days at the marsh when the sky was filled with fast-flying ducks and V-shaped strings of clamoring geese. I discovered a place where I could sit hidden in the tall grass at sunset and watch hundreds of ducks and geese pass just over my head. I saw other birds, too: cranes, hawks, shorebirds, and sometimes even pelicans. Once, I found a heron caught in an animal trap and was able to set it free.

One day, I dressed in old pants and shoes and walked out to the wildest area of the marsh. Suddenly, there was a roar like thunder, as thousands of geese trembled in a huge flock and flapped hard to build speed for a takeoff, then erupted into the air and darkened the sky with their bodies. Meanwhile, far ahead, skimming over the cattails, countless flocks of ducks were crisscrossing in every direction.

I hurried into the water, hardly feeling the winter cold. When the moonless night fell and blended my presence into its darkness, the ducks flew very close. Whirs, whuffles, and whistles passed my ears—exciting!—and ducks landed all around like splashing raindrops.

I sensed a presence overhead and looked up. Hovering just above me was a Great Horned Owl. Seeing me with just my head sticking out of the water, she was trying to decide whether I was something good to eat! Meanwhile, ducks paddled all around, many of them coming so close that I could have reached out and touched them. Later, while I was standing very still in shallow water, one little duck swam nonchalantly between my legs.

The experience was so magical that I completely forgot about myself and the cold. For two or three hours I waded silently from one duck pond to another, using my hands and ears to guide me through the blackness of the night.

Over the years, that very special evening would be followed by many other adventures. At those special times, I discovered how much joy I could feel from being in direct contact with nature. My love for the marshes grew until I felt a great love for all of the natural world.

In my travels, I've found that every part of nature has its own unique gifts to share. Sometimes those gifts are dramatic—like my experience of the water birds at the marsh. At other times they're as quiet as a butterfly landing gently on a flower.

Somewhere near you is a special place where you can have your own experiences of nature's wonders. To help you with your explorations, this book is divided into five sections ("visits"), each one with its own set of stories and things to do.

In Visit One, you'll discover and explore your own special place in nature.

In Visit Two, you'll meet the plants and animals that live there.

Visit Three will help you become aware of the quiet, hidden aspects of nature at your site.

In Visit Four, you'll explore ways to care for your special place. You'll also have a chance to share your discoveries with a friend.

Finally, in Visit Five you'll stay overnight at your special place, or spend the evening and early morning hours there.

As you read the stories and try the activities, you'll develop a connection with the place you've chosen. Through this connection, I believe you'll begin to feel a great love for the earth and a kinship with the animals and plants that live there. I call this experience "touching the heart of nature." To have this experience, it's important that you spend time by yourself out in nature—listening, watching, and waiting for those special times that so few people know because they lack the patience to wait for them.

While hiking in the Sierra Nevada mountains of California, I stopped to rest in a forest clearing where the brush under the trees had been cleared away. The silence made me feel that there might not be any animals living nearby. But I knew that animals hide when they hear humans coming, so I decided to sit quietly and see what would happen.

After fifteen minutes of waiting, my patience was rewarded. Thirty feet from where I sat, two pine martens poked their heads out of their den. (Pine martens are weasels, about the same size as a small domestic cat. They have long, bushy tails and are very quick.)

The martens were young, just a few months old, and they were very curious. At first, they were afraid to leave the safety of their den. But after peering around cautiously, they soon lost their fear and began wrestling and chasing in a wild, playful romp. Now and then, they'd stop to investigate some mysterious new object.

One marten finally noticed me, and with curiosity overcoming caution, came slowly forward to find out what I was. The other young marten followed, then stopped and stared intently from a few feet away. Meanwhile, the brave and inquisitive one came right up and sniffed my leg.

Mother marten, who'd been busy elsewhere, returned and was dismayed to see her children so close to a human being. She rushed forward and, barking *"Come home at once!"* herded her frightened children back to the den.

I was very moved by the trust of the young martens and by the joy I felt while I looked into their beautiful, innocent, curious eyes. I'm sure I was the first human they'd ever seen. Their lack of fear touched my heart and made our meeting memorable. I would have missed the experience if I hadn't stopped to sit quietly until I became part of their world.

Before they set off into the woods, even very experienced hikers make sure someone knows where they're going and when they expect to return. As an important part of your preparation for your journey, you need to ask a parent, Scout leader, teacher, or other adult to act as your guide. He or she will be able to help you by offering suggestions, answering questions, and sharing the enthusiasm of your discoveries. Ask your guide to read this book and help you choose a special place with safe terrain and no dangerous animals or other hazards.

Whether you go alone or take someone with you depends on your age, outdoor experience, preference and the area. (There are many places where traveling alone isn't wise for anyone, regardless of age.) You and your guide can discuss what's the safest and most fun thing you can do.

During each visit you'll find it helpful to bring a pencil (and maybe a notebook), and, if you have them, a magnifying glass and binoculars.

If you'll be going any distance from home or camp, you should consider bringing a watch, jacket or raincoat, small flashlight, whistle, signaling mirror, pocket knife, compass, and some food and water. Remember to tell someone where you're going and when you plan to return.

On the next page, you'll begin your exploration into the *heart of nature. As* you go through the book, remember that you're doing something very important for yourself and for the Earth. For our Earth to survive, it's very important that each of us discover a loving, caring relationship with the natural world around us.

Good luck on your journey!

Choose a place with a variety of plants, animals, and natural features. It's best to choose an area that has several habitats--for example, a place that has woods, fields, and a lake or ocean shore. You'll see more wildlife if your place has three things all animals need to survive: food, shelter, and water.

For some activities, it will help to have a good view of the open sky and the sunset and sunrise, but that isn't essential.

How big should your site be? That's up to you. Some places have natural boundaries: a small valley, for example. Others are bigger than you'd ever be able to explore, like a large forest or a long beach at the ocean. The best area is one you can walk around in two to ten minutes.

Make sure your site is quiet and away from people, so their noise won't distract you. (Don't go so far that getting there and back becomes hard work!) A five- or ten-minute walk is all right. Sometimes, a place that is noisy in the middle of the day is very quiet at dawn or in the early evening.

It's a lot harder to see animals and explore nature when other people are talking, so make sure you're alone when you visit your area. (Exception: In Visit Four you can invite a friend to share your special place.) Of course when you're done with this book, you can take friends to your site whenever you like.

Finding Your Special Place

Since you'll be spending a lot of time at your special place, look for a site that feels good to you--a place you'll enjoy and want to explore.

If you already know a place, check that it meets the guidelines in the list below. If you're not sure which place to choose, explore an area or walk in a direction that you feel might be interesting.

Depending on the surrounding environment, your site might include marshlands, meadows, the ocean, a river or stream, a forest, a lake, or sand dunes.

Finding nature in the city can be more challenging. A natural area like a duck pond in a busy park can give you many wonderful experiences. If you choose a place in the city, try to find a site that has enough plants to attract wild animals and birds.

Wherever you decide to go, look for the best site and then settle in right away. Don't wander around endlessly from place to place. Remember, every site has special features.

Look on the bulletin board for ideas for picking a good site.

What about safety? Even if you feel comfortable being by yourself in nature, it's a good idea to invite your guide along for the first visit, so that he or she knows where your site is located. Remember, on the last visit you have the option of staying overnight. Will you feel comfortable spending the night at this particular site? Make sure to talk about this with your adult guide. Your guide can also help you find out about other things you should know, such as avoiding poisonous plants and wild animals.

You'll want to feel close to the animals at your special place, but it's wise to be careful. It's very dangerous to approach any wild animal too closely, especially if it has young, is sick or wounded, or feels threatened in any way. Avoid animals that are acting in a strange way, since they may have rabies or another disease. If you're careful to avoid dangerous situations, your encounters with animals can be fascinating and safe.

If you are near a populated area, you'll need to talk with your guide about the danger of strangers wandering through your site.

If the site you want to use is on private land, be sure to get the owner's permission. If you're in a park or nature preserve, you'll need to respect their rules. For example, most protected areas won't allow you to collect plants, rocks, and animals.

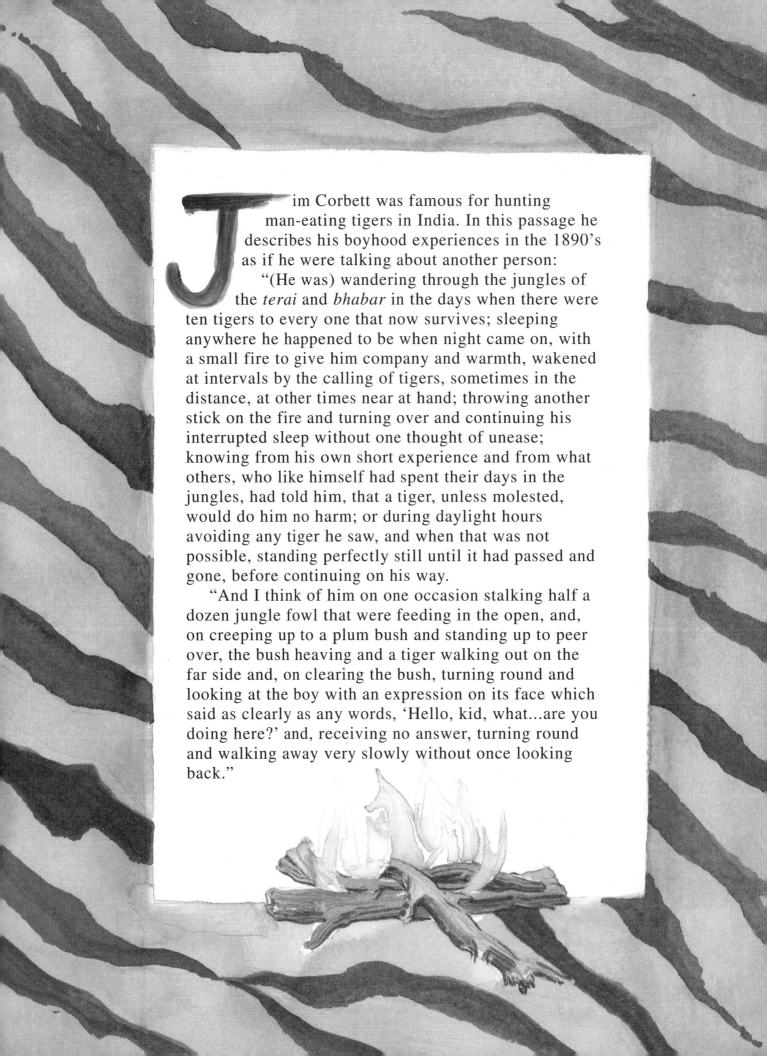

Jim Corbett was famous for hunting man-eating tigers in India. In this passage he describes his boyhood experiences in the 1890's as if he were talking about another person:

"(He was) wandering through the jungles of the *terai* and *bhabar* in the days when there were ten tigers to every one that now survives; sleeping anywhere he happened to be when night came on, with a small fire to give him company and warmth, wakened at intervals by the calling of tigers, sometimes in the distance, at other times near at hand; throwing another stick on the fire and turning over and continuing his interrupted sleep without one thought of unease; knowing from his own short experience and from what others, who like himself had spent their days in the jungles, had told him, that a tiger, unless molested, would do him no harm; or during daylight hours avoiding any tiger he saw, and when that was not possible, standing perfectly still until it had passed and gone, before continuing on his way.

"And I think of him on one occasion stalking half a dozen jungle fowl that were feeding in the open, and, on creeping up to a plum bush and standing up to peer over, the bush heaving and a tiger walking out on the far side and, on clearing the bush, turning round and looking at the boy with an expression on its face which said as clearly as any words, 'Hello, kid, what...are you doing here?' and, receiving no answer, turning round and walking away very slowly without once looking back."

First Impressions

After choosing a special site, take time to wander around and just have fun. Then pick a comfortable spot where you can think about the area and answer these questions.

What are some of the first things you noticed about your site?

How do you feel being here?

Pick a name that suits your special place. You can change it later, if you think of something better. But naming it at the start will help you make the site your own right away.

The name of my site is:

Mapping the Boundaries of Your Site

Draw a map of your site as it might appear to a hawk flying overhead. Take a walk around the edges of the area, and use the space above to draw any existing trails or special landmarks (big rocks, ponds, flowering bushes, and so on). For now, just concentrate on sketching the general shape of the site, using the entire space, and leaving plenty of room for smaller features that you can add later.

The Adventure Hunt

Most people learn about their surroundings using only their eyes. But it's lots of fun to explore with the other senses, too. In this activity, you'll use sight, hearing, touch and smell to make new discoveries.

A) Find the best view and give that place a special name. Mark its location on your map, then sketch the view in the space below. Later, you'll share the sketch with a friend.

B) Find the best place to listen for nature sounds. Then, see how long it takes to hear at least five different sounds. Name this place and mark it on your map. See if you can figure out what is making the sounds.

Write down the sounds:

1)

2)

3)

4)

5)

C) Describe a bird's call or any other natural sound that you hear, using words or letters. For example, the gathering call of the California Quail has been described as "Chi-*ca*'-go!" or "Come-*right*-here!" and the sound of a seal as "Arhk, Arhk."

The sound you heard:

D) Use your hands to find the warmest and coldest places and mark each of them on the map. How might these places change during the night?

Warmest place(s):   Coldest place(s):

 E) Stop at different places. Close your eyes and focus your attention on the sense of smell. Find two different smells and describe them. See if you can figure out where they come from.

1)

2)

As you walked around your site, you probably noticed some places that were especially interesting. In exploring these areas, we'll refer to them as "neighborhoods."

To explore in the best possible way, slow down and look at everything with deep interest and attention. The famous painter, Claude Monet, saw small details in nature that most people would probably overlook. His ability to see so clearly enabled Monet to create many beautiful paintings from subjects in his small garden at Giverny, France. The brilliant colors of the flowers, the play of light and shadow, and the changing seasons made his garden look very different at different times of the day and year.

Move through your site slowly, looking for places that have unique qualities. You might see a group of noisy frogs, for example, or a shady grove of trees, or a colony of ants, or a place where the wind is very strong. When you find such a place, try these activities:

A) Many Native North Americans practiced "Still Hunting." To try this fascinating practice in your site, approach the area as quietly as you can, moving slowly and trying not to step on dry leaves or twigs. Find a place where you'll be partly hidden by bushes or trees, then sit and remain perfectly still for at least ten minutes. As you sit quietly and blend into your surroundings, the animals will once again resume their natural activity.

Enjoy the nearby plants dancing with the wind, the butterflies fluttering past, and the birds calling. Watch as the "little world" all around you comes back to life. You may even have the thrilling experience of watching a bird or other animal from just a few feet away.

B) After experiencing how nature lives when there are no humans around, try different ways of interacting with the site. Does talking to the frogs make them be quiet? (John Muir used to "entertain" squirrels by singing to them!) See if you can imitate the sounds of the animals you hear. Can you get them to answer? If there are no large animals, find out what happens when you place a twig or rock across the path of some ants; or see if you can get any of the plants to respond to your touch.

C) Choose the three most interesting "neighborhoods" to write about. Name each place after its most interesting feature—for example, Frog Bluff, Ant Rock, or Windy Point. Then draw it on the map that you created for the Mapping the Boundaries activity on page 20.

Write down some of your thoughts for each location, and describe some of the things you observed with your different senses. You could answer questions like these: What makes this place unique? What special things happen here? How does the site make me feel?

Neighborhoods

SHADY GROVE

FROG BLUFF

GOPHER GULCH

WINDY POINT TRAIL

Neighborhood #1: (name) _____

Neighborhood #2: (name) _____

Neighborhood #3: (name) _____

"For observing nature, the best pace is a snail's pace."

–Edwin Way Teale

George Washington Carver was born into slavery in 1864, and was orphaned before age two. Despite these enormous handicaps, he became one of the greatest scientists of the twentieth century.

As a boy, George was curious about everything. He wanted to know where the sun went at night, and what made the rain fall. He wondered why one rose was yellow and another one was red. When he was still very young, he discovered that he could often get the answers directly from nature, just by visiting his secret places.

Throughout his life, George kept asking questions. In his adult years, he was known as "The Wizard of Tuskegee" because of his ability to find answers to questions that no one else could answer. (Tuskegee was the first African-American college in the United States.) George said that nature was like one giant broadcasting station, and that if you listened carefully enough she would reveal her secrets.

Choose one special area of your site and use your curiosity to discover the rich detail that lies hidden there. If you find dew on the plants, for example, you might wonder:

- Where does the dew come from?
- Why is there dew in some places but not others?
- Does the dew disappear at the same time every day?

Or, you might have questions like the following:

- Where are the birds going when they fly overhead?
- Where did they come from?
- How can this bush live in such dry soil?
- Why does this kind of tree grow only in the shade?
- Where did all the shells on this beach come from?

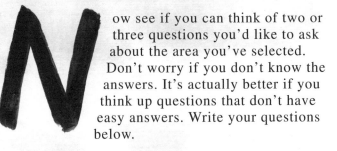

Now see if you can think of two or three questions you'd like to ask about the area you've selected. Don't worry if you don't know the answers. It's actually better if you think up questions that don't have easy answers. Write your questions below.

Choose a question that makes you particularly curious. Write down an answer that makes sense to you.

You probably chose this place because of its beauty and wildness. It's also special because of its animals and plants, many of which have lived here for hundreds or even thousands of years.

You can show your appreciation for this area by helping to preserve its beauty and naturalness. If you are careful and pick up after yourself, no one will ever know you've been here. If you see signs left behind by other human visitors, try to restore the area's wildness. For example, you could dismantle any unnecessary campfire rings or remove any litter.

Awakening Curiosity

2

Second Visit

One Big Family

A friend of mine named Wyatt worked for a while as caretaker at a big fruit orchard in central Washington. As he went about his work, he saw that many birds made the orchard their home. Gradually, he learned to make friends with the birds. At first he made mistakes, like teasing the meadowlarks by whistling and mimicking their songs. They simply ignored his antics and made sharp, chirping noises. But when he spoke quietly to them, he found that they answered with soft singing sounds.

One morning while Wyatt was watering, a pair of robins began making a tremendous racket in a tree nearby. When he walked over to investigate, he saw that the birds' nest was being drenched by a sprinkler, so he quickly walked back and turned down the water.

A few days later, two small birds flew up and fluttered around his head. At first this made him just a little bit curious, but as he returned to his work the birds became even more agitated. Finally Wyatt realized that the birds wanted to show him something, so he followed them a hundred yards to the far side of the orchard.

Arriving at one of the trees, the birds flew high up in the branches. Climbing after them as fast as he could, Wyatt discovered a big snake that had just raided the birds' nest. Unfortunately, Wyatt hadn't understood the birds' plight in time to save their young.

Wyatt was deeply touched that the birds had come to him for help. From then on, he took his responsibilities as "Protector of the Orchard" seriously.

There are many stories similar to this one, that show the wonderful relationship that humans and animals can enjoy. Yet the only time most people ever see a wild animal is when it runs away. The reason is that people make lots of noise when they're outdoors. But when people relate to animals in a quiet, friendly way, the results are often thrilling.

During this visit, you'll have a chance to start developing friendships with the animals that live at your site. Depending on the area and time of day, you might see many animals right away, or you might have to start by looking for tracks, droppings, feathers, and other animal signs. (Early morning and evening are usually the best times to see birds and mammals.) When you find animal tracks, follow them. Bird droppings or feathers often mean a nest is nearby.

Remember that insects are animals, too! Their lives are amazing, and you'll probably be able to observe them more easily than birds and mammals.

The Black Fly larva lives in the fast-flowing streams. To keep from being carried away by the water, it has a suction cup at the end of its body that holds it firmly in place. Even if the fly larva does get swept away, it doesn't go far, because it has a "safety rope" made of silken thread that it uses to crawl back to its original position. Black Flies grow to adult size while still underwater. To keep their wings from getting wet, they ride to the water's surface inside a bubble of air, like tiny submarines!

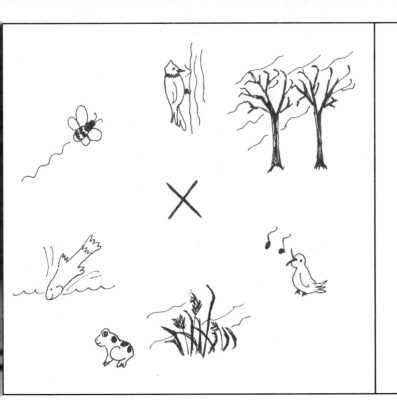

Creating a Sound Map

We can often hear animals before we see them. A good way to know if animals are around is to listen for their calls and the sounds of their movements. Go to the place where you think you'll be able to hear the greatest variety of animal sounds. Then close your eyes and listen with deep attention for sounds such as...

The drumming of a woodpecker... The buzzing of a fly... Wind rushing through the treetops... Water cascading and singing down a steep, rocky ravine... An unknown bird calling deep in the forest....

In the space above you are going to draw a "Sound Map." Place an X in the center of the space to show where you are sitting. Then, for each sound you hear, draw a mark on the map that shows how far away the sound is and the direction. See if you can draw marks that look like the sounds. Make the marks very simple—for example, two wavy lines for the wind, or a musical note for a songbird.

Experiment with using your hands as "kangaroo ears." Cup your hands behind your ears to help you hear sounds more clearly. (Your cupped hands make a larger surface that reflects more sound into your ears.) Turn the "cups" backward and listen for sounds behind you. It generally takes 5-10 minutes of sitting and listening to make a good Sound Map.

How many different sounds did you hear?

What animals did you hear?

Describe the animal sounds you couldn't identify:

Reading the Forest

Tom Brown Jr. is a well-known American tracker and naturalist who was trained by an Apache Indian named Stalking Wolf. Tom Brown said that Stalking Wolf always knew what was going on in the forest, because he was constantly listening to the sounds of birds and squirrels and other animals. A snake or other predator often will cause small animals to become silent or to begin chattering. Stalking Wolf could identify and track a predator from a hundred yards away, just by listening to the animals nearby and how they reacted to the alarm calls of animals farther away.

Animals live together in a "community," and are always affecting one another through their actions. Listen again for animal sounds. This time, see if you can notice animals interacting with each other. For example, did you hear birds singing the same song back and forth? Or a mother bird calling and gathering her young? Or animals responding to another animal's alarm call or movements? If you didn't hear anything, keeep alert for sounds diring the rest of the visit.

Who Lives Here?

Seeing animals is one of the most exciting things you can experience at your site. Still Hunting, on page 24, and the following activities can help you enter into the "little worlds" of nature.

Earth Windows: Find a place where there are trees towering above you. Lie down on your back and cover yourself with pine needles, leaves, long grass, and other natural materials until only your eyes are showing. (Make sure to shake any dirt out of the leaves before you cover your face!)

Feel that you are looking up through the forest floor. Enjoy the blue sky...the swaying branches...the passing clouds. Lie still for at least 10 minutes. Hidden under the forest floor, maybe you'll get lucky and an animal will come close to you. (Don't use this exercise in an area that has ticks, red ants, and other biting or stinging insects.)

Barefoot Stalking: Take off your shoes and socks and walk as slowly and quietly as you can. Test each step before putting your full weight on the ground, to avoid crackling leaves and twigs.

Bird Calling: If you hear small birds in your area, stand or sit very still near some bushes or trees, then repeat the sound *"pssh"* several times in sets of four: *"pssh... pssh... pssh... pssh."* Repeat the four-part call three to five times, then do several more sets of calls and wait to see what happens. Curious birds will often come looking for the source of the noise. Many times I've been visited by as many as fifty birds after using this call. The birds will either respond in a few minutes or not at all. (I've had great success with this bird call in North America and to some extent in Europe.)

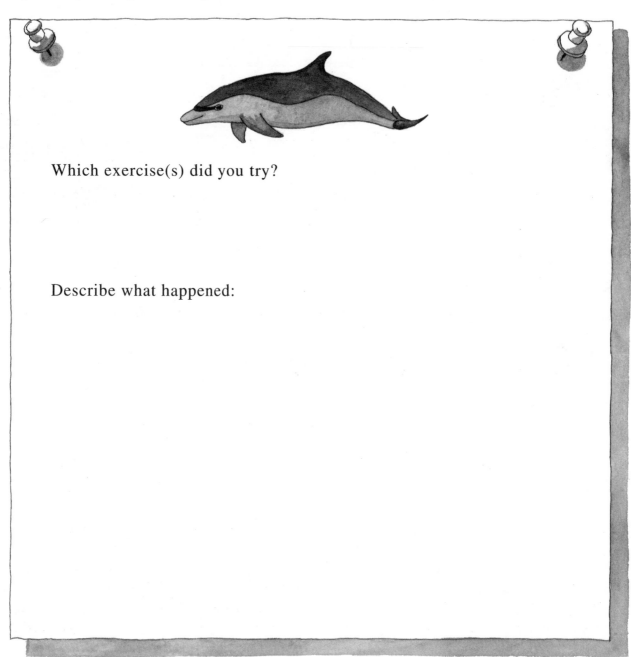

Which exercise(s) did you try?

Describe what happened:

ATTRACTING ANIMALS

Animals need shelter, food, and water. Look around your area and see if any of these necessities of life are missing. The following example tells how the animals near my home responded when I supplied one of their needs.

Where I live, there is very little rain in summer, so I set out basins of water where the birds can drink and bathe. But every night the deer come and drink from the bird baths, leaving the basins dry.

In the morning, a little gathering of local birds and squirrels are usually waiting in the trees and bushes near my house. When I come out, they fly and scamper in from all directions. Gradually I've gotten to know some of them as individuals. One particularly friendly bird hops along the ground under the bird bath. When it sees me, it flies up and sits on the bird bath and looks at me as if to say, "Hey, I need some water!" Then it flies to a nearby branch while I fill the basin. As soon as I finish and begin to leave, it flies down for a drink and a bath.

Here are two things you can do to help the animals in your area:

Brush Piles

To create a safe home for small animals, make a brush pile. For best results, choose a place where the animals can find food and water nearby, and where there isn't any other shelter. A good place is a meadow or open forest floor.

Place logs and larger limbs on the bottom to keep the pile from matting down to the ground, then stack brush up to a height of four or five feet, making the pile at least twice as wide as it is high. Finally, put some heavier limbs on top of the brush to keep everything in place. Use only dead materials like fallen logs, slash wood left over from logging, or even old Christmas trees.

Water Basins

Put out a dish or basin and keep it filled with water. The best type of container is about 2" deep, with gently sloping sides that give the birds a foothold as they enter the water. If your container is deeper than 2", you can put rocks in it for the birds to stand on.

Place the container in an open area so the birds can easily see cats and other approaching predators. Nearby shrubs or trees give the birds a place to escape to and a sense of security. In dry climates, it's especially important to keep the basin filled, because the birds will begin to rely on it. You'll be amazed at the number and variety of birds that will come to drink and bathe.

What did you do to help the animals?

_____
_____
_____
_____
_____
_____
_____
_____

Did you see any evidence that the animals responded? (You may have to wait a day or more to answer this question.)

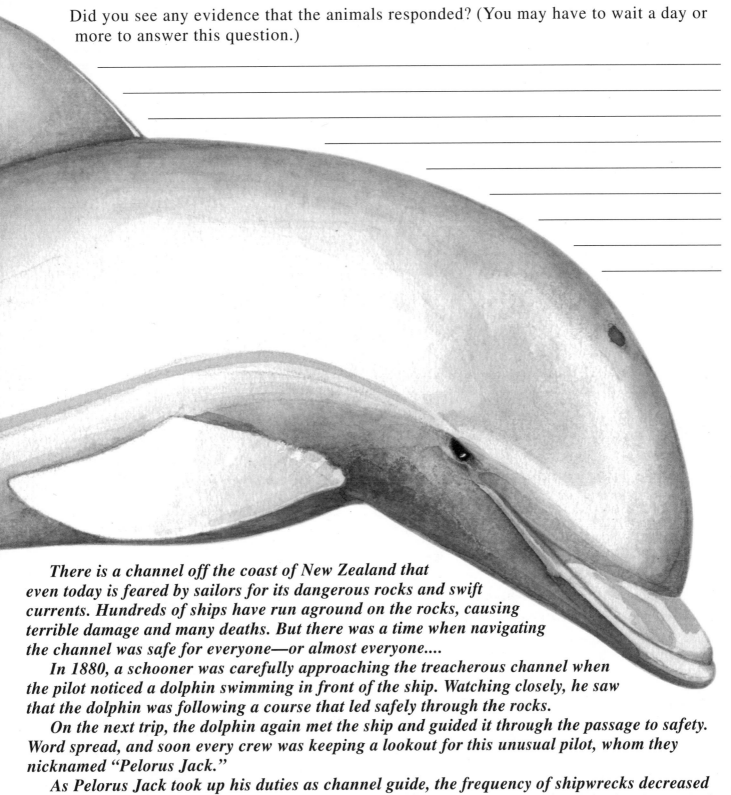

There is a channel off the coast of New Zealand that even today is feared by sailors for its dangerous rocks and swift currents. Hundreds of ships have run aground on the rocks, causing terrible damage and many deaths. But there was a time when navigating the channel was safe for everyone—or almost everyone....

In 1880, a schooner was carefully approaching the treacherous channel when the pilot noticed a dolphin swimming in front of the ship. Watching closely, he saw that the dolphin was following a course that led safely through the rocks.

On the next trip, the dolphin again met the ship and guided it through the passage to safety. Word spread, and soon every crew was keeping a lookout for this unusual pilot, whom they nicknamed "Pelorus Jack."

As Pelorus Jack took up his duties as channel guide, the frequency of shipwrecks decreased dramatically. One night a ship called the S.S. Penguin came into the channel, and Pelorus Jack appeared as usual to lead the way. Unfortunately, a drunken sailor thought it would be "fun" to use the dolphin for target practice. He fired a few shots and there was a great thrashing in the water, then Pelorus Jack was seen swimming away trailing a stream of blood.

For weeks, no one saw the dolphin. Then one day he reappeared, healthy again and just as willing to lead ships safely through the passage...with one exception. Whenever the S.S. Penguin came through the channel, Pelorus Jack was nowhere in sight. Interestingly, the Penguin was later wrecked while sailing through the area that Pelorus Jack patrolled.

When Ohiyesa, a Santee Dakota Indian boy, left his tipi each morning, his uncle would say, "Look closely at everything you see." When Ohiyesa returned in the evening, his uncle often questioned him about what he saw.

"It was his custom to let me name all the new birds that I had seen during the day. I would name them according to the color or the shape of the bill or their song or the appearance and locality of the nest—in fact anything about the bird that impressed me...I made many ridiculous errors, I must admit."

Yet whenever Ohiyesa's careful observation allowed him to describe a bird accurately, his uncle warmly praised him.

Ohiyesa was taught to think of all animals as his close relatives. His tribe, like most Indians, saw no real separation between themselves and animals. In fact, animals were generally regarded as being wise teachers and elders, because one could learn so much from observing them. Instead of referring to dragonflies, salmon, mice, and bats as "animals," many Native North Americans today prefer to call them "all our relations."

Observe carefully some of the animals that visit or live in your special area. In the space below, list the animals you see, but don't worry if you don't know their names. For now, just make up your own names. Later, after observing them closely, you can ask someone their names, or look them up in a book.

List the animals you saw:

Choose an animal that you can observe easily, but know little about. See if you can answer the following questions:

A) What is its size?

B) What are its colorings and markings?

C) How does it move? (fly, crawl, jump, run, etc.)

D) Where did you see it? (tree canopy, stream, open ground, etc.)

E) What was it doing? Was it alone or with others?

F) What does it eat?

All Our Relations

G) Did it make any sounds? Describe.

H) Did it notice you?

I) What name do you want to give it?

While watching the gray tree squirrels near my home, I've come to know several of them as individuals. A big male with a pink patch on its upper chest seems to be the dominant squirrel, because he drives the others away. When he sees another squirrel, he stands tall on his hind feet and rears back, then leaps forward in a mad rush. I call him "Chaser." While watching Chaser and his friends, I've discovered the "tree highways" the squirrels use to avoid enemies like bobcats and large hawks...

knowledge of African birds. Helen looked through the book until she found the bird she thought the Masai were mimicking. Five delighted smiles told Helen her guess was right.

Besides knowing the behavior of every animal that lives nearby, many native people are aware of individual animals, too. For example, a native hunter might be able to distinguish a particular deer or gazelle by its track, special markings, shape of its antlers or horns, or scars showing where it has been injured.

In this activity, you'll try to identify an individual animal by its unique characteristics. See if you can get to know this animal well enough to pick it out from others of its kind. Try to find it each time you visit your area.

Helen, a student in one of my teacher workshops, told me a delightful story from a bird-watching trip to Kenya, Africa. She was standing with a couple of friends at a trail crossing, when five Masai tribesmen walked up. Helen wanted to ask them if a certain bird lived nearby, but she couldn't speak their language.

She flipped through her bird book and showed the Masai a picture of the bird she wanted to see. The Masai men smiled and began to imitate the bird's behavior. Then they pointed to where it could be found. The bird-watchers, thrilled to have such knowledgeable guides, showed the Masai several more pictures. The Masai mimicked each bird's mannerisms and pointed to its likely whereabouts. Helen was amazed at how well the Masai knew the local birds.

Then the Masai selected their own bird and began acting it out. Now it was the bird-watchers' turn to demonstrate their

Make sure the animal you choose is one you can observe in detail and that you think you'll see often. Animals like deer and rabbits are good choices because they remain in the same general area. If there is a pond or stream in your area, you might see if you can identify a particular frog, fish, or turtle. You may have to look at several animals before you find one you can easily identify. (Use binoculars, if you have them, to get a close look at the animal.)

If you have trouble picking out an individual animal, try to find an active nest or den and watch the animals there. Be careful not to disturb birds that are nesting or roosting, and avoid coming so close to an animal that it feels threatened. (Even animals that appear harmless, such as deer, can be dangerous if approached too closely.)

Hello there ...I know you.

Write down the type of the animal you chose, and describe how you were able to pick it out from others of its kind. Give the animal a special name, based on its markings, color, size, behavior, and so on. Did you discover anything new about this animal's habits?

Kind of animal:

Special characteristics:

Did you learn anything new about the animal?

Individual's Name:

If you see your special animal again on a later visit, check below:

❑ Visit Three ❑ Visit Four ❑ Visit Five

The Web of Life at Your Site

The animals, plants, rocks, and soil of an area form a community of living and non-living things that depend on each other:

The shadow of a tree provides a perfect place for shade-loving plants to grow.

The roots of some trees depend on soil fungi to help them gather nutrients from the earth.

Rain, or lack of rain, can be influenced by nearby mountains.

Plants and animals die and become food for other plants and animals.

Everything in nature is influenced by the many other things living nearby.

Choose eleven things from your site that you've seen—or seen signs of. Write a name in each of the circles to the right. (Make sure to include some plants and animals and even a few physical features—like rocks, soil, and a mountain.) Draw lines from one circle to everything it influences or is influenced by. For example, a mouse could have lines drawn to a flea, a log, grass, and a hawk. Then draw lines from the other ten circles. You now have a web of life for your site.

Pretend that one of the things you put in a circle has disappeared from the site. For example, a tree is cut down, or a stream dries up. Scientists have discovered that if you remove the dead or dying trees from a forest, one fifth of the animals may lose their homes. Cover that circle and follow its lines to see how many other things are affected.

Which circle did you cover?

Which things were affected when it disappeared?

Is there something in your site that is not affected by anything else?

"When we try to pick out anything by itself, we find it hitched to everything else in the universe."

–John Muir

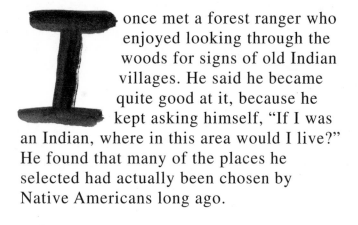

I once met a forest ranger who enjoyed looking through the woods for signs of old Indian villages. He said he became quite good at it, because he kept asking himself, "If I was an Indian, where in this area would I live?" He found that many of the places he selected had actually been chosen by Native Americans long ago.

Imagine people living in your site a thousand years ago. Did the land look different then? Where would people build their homes? Where could they find food and water and materials for building? Is there a place you think would be warmer in winter or cooler in summer?

Look around your site for signs of ancient and more recent human use. You might find evidence that is obvious, like a tree stump, an old building foundation, or an abandoned fruit orchard. Other signs can be more subtle, like a level area on a steep hillside, or a small pit or mound.

If you find something unusual, try to figure out what it is. One day while I was walking through a forest I noticed a long flat area among the trees. After looking at it more closely and tracing its course, I found I had discovered an old wagon road.

Clues to the Past

Write down any signs of past human use you discover:

I N THE EARLY YEARS OF THIS CENTURY, a Japanese
Buddhist monk named Godo Nakanishi devoted his life
to practicing inner calmness and compassion for all creatures. As time
passed, Godo's appreciation of nature grew stronger, especially for the birds.
Godo even created a new word, *yacho*, which means "wild bird." 🐦 Godo
once spent several days sitting quietly on a snow-covered mountain. A flock of
wild birds noticed him, but their fear of humans kept them in the tree branches a
safe distance away. 🐦 Godo continued to sit quietly. Gradually, the birds came
closer, their fear melting in the peace they felt from the monk.

Getting Close to Nature

3

Third Visit

In time, they accepted him as a trusted friend and perched on his shoulders and knees. ➤ In 1934, Godo Nakanishi created the Wild Bird Society of Japan. He spent over 50 years promoting nature conservation. When Godo died, a flycatcher bird perched quietly on his window sill and gazed at his face. And just before the funeral procession, a Japanese kestrel was seen flying in circles over his head as if in silent farewell. ➤ In this story, we see how Godo Nakanishi's quality of peace earned the animals' trust. In many countries, stories are told about animals that are drawn to people who are calm and have kindly thoughts.

A friend of mine named Maria told me how she made friends with a family of beavers. While backpacking in the Rocky Mountains of Colorado, she came to a beautiful lake and began to set up camp. A beaver in the lake became alarmed and began slapping its flat tail loudly on the water to warn its family. For the rest of the day, the beavers carefully avoided Maria's side of the lake.

Maria spent the day sitting by the lake, enjoying the peace of the surroundings and watching the play of light and wind on the water. The next morning, a pair of beavers cautiously swam by for a closer look. As they passed where she was sitting, the two brave beavers turned their heads and watched her carefully. Apparently they decided that Maria could be trusted, because soon the beaver family came to feed on Maria's side of the lake, allowing her to observe them quietly.

As you learned during the earlier visits, the first step in gaining the trust of animals is to move slowly and quietly—or better yet, to sit completely still. The second step is more challenging. Animals can sense how we feel toward them and whether we mean them harm. Before they'll trust us, they must sense that our intentions are peaceful and kindly.

Allen Boone wrote several books about his experiences with animals. In *The Language of Silence*, Boone describes an experience with wild monkeys.

While exploring a jungle trail, Boone stopped in a beautiful clearing to relax and enjoy the surroundings. A few minutes later his rest was interrupted when a big monkey dropped out of a tree and approached him cautiously. Stopping a safe distance away, the monkey sat down and studied the intruder. Remaining calmly seated, Boone sent thoughts of peace and friendship to the monkey. After some minutes, the monkey got up and gazed slowly around the clearing, signaling that Boone had passed "inspection."

Boone describes what happened next:

"Within the next few minutes the clearing became alive with monkeys. Never had I ever witnessed a spectacle like it...There were big ones and little ones. Old monkeys, middle-aged ones, and babies that had to be carried. Groups of them, as well as aloners. Some of them were chattering loudly, others were completely silent. They came dropping down from the trees—*it was raining monkeys!*"

Boone watched the monkeys for several hours, during which none showed the slightest sign of fear.

At one point, the monkeys suddenly looked south, then fled in alarm. Curious to find out what had frightened the monkeys, Boone remained in the clearing. After three hours of waiting, he heard human voices approaching from the south. When the party arrived, they announced that they were hunters, and that they'd heard there was good monkey hunting in that particular clearing. They were feeling discouraged because they had not seen a monkey all day.

Remembering the monkeys' sudden flight, Boon asked the hunters when they'd set out on their hunt. The men said they had started three hours ago, exactly the time the monkeys fled the clearing.

Friendly encounters with wild animals are treasured moments. When we are relaxed and peaceful, animals relax and feel comfortable in our presence, even to the extent of approaching closely. The following two activities can help you to become quiet and to feel a sense of harmony with your surroundings.

To get close to an animal, speak softly and tell it you mean no harm. Tell the animal how much you admire it. It won't be able to understand your words, but it will understand your intentions. Stay in the area long enough for the animal to get used to your presence. In time it will come to accept you.

The Listening Game

Listen to the symphony of sounds at your site. Gradually focus your attention until you are listening to just one sound. For example, if there is a stream in the area, find a place where the water is tumbling over rocks with bubbling, gurgling sounds. Listen for at least thirty seconds, then choose one small part of the stream and listen just to the sounds coming from that place. Finally, choose a little cascade or waterfall and focus on the noise made by that one tiny part of the stream. (You may need to get very close to the water.) Similarly, you can listen to waves lapping on the shore of a lake or crashing on a sandy ocean beach.

Another good practice is to listen to the leaves of a tree fluttering in the wind. First, listen to the sound made by all the leaves and branches; then focus on the sounds coming from just one branch. (Can you pick out your tree's "song" from the songs of other trees?) Finally, move right up close to the tree, or climb it, and see if you can hear the sound of just one leaf rustling in the wind.

You can even use the Listening Game in the desert, or other places where there are no trees or streams. Just listen to all the sounds, especially those in the far distance, then gradually shift your attention to nearby sounds like insects, or the sand being blown by the wind.

Describe what you hear:

"With

There is a fable about two traveling dogs who came to a small town. One dog, finding the front door of a building open, boldly walked in for a look. To its surprise, it saw 100 snarling dogs. Frightened, it fled the building.

A little later, the second dog, unaware of what had happened to its friend, discovered the same open door and happily went inside. To its delight, this dog saw 100 smiling dogs, all wagging their tails.

Why was the experience of the second dog so different from that of the first? The answer is that the room was filled with 100 mirrors and each dog saw its own reflection 100 times. The first dog, mistrusting the other dogs, snarled to defend itself, while the second dog, expecting the other dogs to be friendly, happily greeted them and thus received 100 friendly greetings in return.

Like the mirrors in the story, the world reflects our thoughts back to us. How we think affects how we experience the world.

Ralph Waldo Emerson, the famous 19th century American philosopher, spent his whole life looking for good and noble things in life. He took great delight in nature, and expressed his joy for living by saying, "This world is so beautiful that I can hardly believe it exists."

This world truly is a beautiful place, if our eyes are open to see it. The following activity will help you find the special beauty that's in your place.

Begin by memorizing the Navajo poem *With Beauty Before Me*. It's very easy to remember; just think about the six directions: "before and behind," "above and below," "around and within."

With beauty before me, may I walk.

With beauty behind me, may I walk.

With beauty above me, may I walk.

With beauty below me, may I walk.

With beauty all around me, may I walk.

Wandering on a trail of beauty, lively I walk. [*]

[*]Music for this poem is available on the audio cassette tape *A Day in the Forest,* from Dawn Publications.

Beauty Before Me"

An easy way to learn the words to the poem is to close your eyes and take three steps forward while you repeat the first line. Stop and open your eyes, then look straight ahead and see what beautiful object first catches your attention. Close your eyes again and take three more steps while you repeat the next line. Turn around, open your eyes, and find something beautiful behind you. Repeat this for each line, looking above, below, and all around.

On the last line, keep your eyes closed and try to feel the beauty within yourself. When you're finished, record what you saw in each direction.

With beauty before me...

With beauty behind me...

With beauty above me...

With beauty below me...

With beauty all around me...

Wandering on a trail of beauty, lively I walk. (Feel beauty inside.)

For the Navajos, another meaning of "beauty" is harmony. As you walk, feel a sense of harmony with the nearby plants... animals... rocks... and sky.

Now walk slowly through your area with eyes open. Quietly continue to repeat the poem, enjoying the beauty of the clouds, grasses, trees, and hills, and whatever else comes to your attention.

Now that you've gotten to know some of the animals, plants, and physical features of your site, it might be fun to pick a special name for yourself that you can use during your visits. Choose the one thing in your site that you're most attracted to. Have you found a tall tree that rises above its neighbors? Or a brightly colored bird or flower? Or an insect that amazes you with its ability to jump, swim, or fly?

Where I live in northern California, I enjoy watching the Canyon Wrens—stocky little rusty-brown birds that are very active and curious. These wrens live in canyons, caves and cliff areas where there is lots of water. You can hear their loud, musical song long before you see them. Their zestful *te te te te tew tew tew tew* call starts high then descends like a staircase and is easily heard as it echoes off the canyon walls. For me, the Canyon Wrens express the quality of happiness, so I once chose the Earth Name "Laughing Wren in the Canyon."

Think about the plant, animal or physical feature you've chosen, and the quality it represents. For example a mountain peak might inspire you to feel strong and courageous. The quality can be one you already have, or one you admire and want to strengthen in yourself. You can combine the name with one or more words that describe the quality. Some examples are "Swift Hawk," "Singing River," and "Bright Moon." During Visit Four you can share your Earth Name with a friend.

My Earth Name is:

Choosing an Earth Name

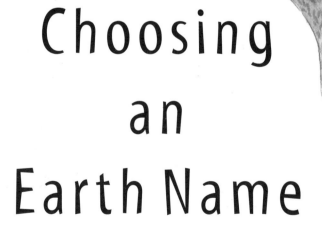

Once upon a time, there was a wise man who lived in the wilderness. One day, a visitor asked him how he had learned so much about life, living all by himself.

He said, "Nature has been my teacher. Most of the truly important lessons in life I learned by carefully studying the rocks, plants, and animals. Let me share with you four important lessons I have learned.

"The first lesson is about being helpful to others. If you look closely, you will see that everything in nature is linked to everything else. How can the trees grow without the sun? How can the birds live without trees? How can frogs survive without ponds? If only we humans would learn to be more helpful to the plants, animals, and each other, then the world would become a place of beauty and harmony.

"The second lesson is about enthusiasm, for without enthusiasm it is impossible to accomplish anything worthwhile in life. My teachers have been the young animals. They do everything with so much energy!—Whether they are eating, exploring, or playing. The more I watched, the more I realized that their energy and enthusiasm made their lives a joy. In this way, I learned that if I, too, want to enjoy life, I need to keep my enthusiasm high.

"The third lesson is about perseverance and to keep trying, no matter what difficulties we face. This lesson I learned from the spiders. Have you watched them spin their webs? If a gust of wind or a passing animal tears the web down, the spider goes right back to work. In this way, I learned not to waste time and energy feeling bad when things go wrong, but to just get started again.

"The last lesson is about discrimination, and how to choose between things that can help or hurt us. The honey bees taught me this lesson. As they go about their work collecting pollen, they fly straight to the beautiful flowers—you never see them land on rotten or unclean things. In this way, I learned to make choices in life that bring lasting happiness, and to avoid things that lead to suffering and pain."

Like the wise man in the story, look around your site and see if there are any lessons you can learn from nature. A rock might teach you about patience or firmness. Ants might demonstrate cooperation or determination. Choose two things you feel particularly drawn to. Look at each one carefully and try to see what quality it represents for you. Write down your answers.

Name of your first choice:

What can your learn from it?

Learning from Nature

"We have always considered our wild animals a symbol of freedom. Nothing holds them back. They run free. So, you see, without them something is missing from even the most beautiful landscape. The land becomes empty, and only with the presence of wild living things can it gain full beauty."

–The Dalai Lama of Tibet

Name of your second choice:

What can you learn from it?

The Poetry of

Writing a poem is another way to become more aware of your site. Choose a favorite place and sit for a few minutes watching and enjoying. Notice how each sound, movement, texture and color is different. Feel the special quality that each thing expresses. If you see a darting, swift-moving flock of birds, feel in your heart the joy of their flight. If you see a tree swaying in a light breeze, feel its strength and gracefulness. Try one of the following forms of poetry, or any other style you like.

Vertical Poem

Choose a word that captures the feeling of the place you've chosen. Then use each letter of the word to begin a line of your poem. While walking on Mount Subasio near Assisi, Italy, I wrote a poem to the word "spring." The flower-covered hillsides expressed a feeling of excitement as the shadows of the clouds raced over them.

S un-made cloud shadows

P laced on the earth

R unning across its surface

I n and out of the sun I sit

N ot long does the cloud's twin stay

G oing, going on its way.

Now write the word you've chosen, with one letter on each line. Then use each letter to begin a line of your poem.

— _____

— _____

— _____

— _____

— _____

— _____

— _____

Haiku

Japanese Haiku is a form of poetry with only three lines. The first line contains five syllables, the second line has seven, and the third line has five again. Look for the syllables in the Haiku poem below.

  1 2   3 4   5
In the sudden burst
  Of summer rain...wind-blown birds
Clutching at grasses
–Buson

Also, in Haiku poetry, the first two lines describe the scene and the third line expresses surprise or discovery. The two poems to the right are by Basho, another famous master of Haiku.

Your Site

An old silent pond
  Into the pond a frog jumps,
Splash! silence again

My eyes following
  Until a bird was lost at sea
Found a small island

My Haiku Poem:

Fourth Visit

Caring
For Your
Site

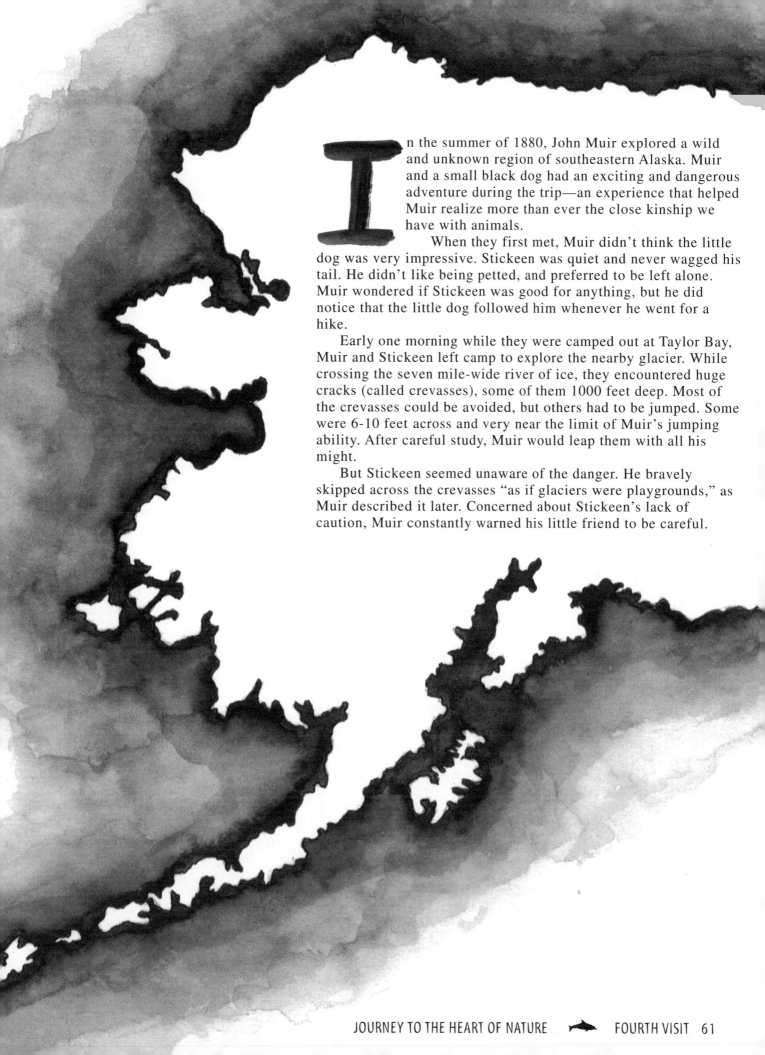

In the summer of 1880, John Muir explored a wild and unknown region of southeastern Alaska. Muir and a small black dog had an exciting and dangerous adventure during the trip—an experience that helped Muir realize more than ever the close kinship we have with animals.

When they first met, Muir didn't think the little dog was very impressive. Stickeen was quiet and never wagged his tail. He didn't like being petted, and preferred to be left alone. Muir wondered if Stickeen was good for anything, but he did notice that the little dog followed him whenever he went for a hike.

Early one morning while they were camped out at Taylor Bay, Muir and Stickeen left camp to explore the nearby glacier. While crossing the seven mile-wide river of ice, they encountered huge cracks (called crevasses), some of them 1000 feet deep. Most of the crevasses could be avoided, but others had to be jumped. Some were 6-10 feet across and very near the limit of Muir's jumping ability. After careful study, Muir would leap them with all his might.

But Stickeen seemed unaware of the danger. He bravely skipped across the crevasses "as if glaciers were playgrounds," as Muir described it later. Concerned about Stickeen's lack of caution, Muir constantly warned his little friend to be careful.

Muir and Stickeen eventually reached the far shore, and then, hours later, began the return journey across the ice. It looked like the route Muir chose would be easy—until they came to a 50-foot-wide crevasse that stopped them in their tracks. Muir searched hard but couldn't find a way around or over the crevasse. The only crossing place was so dangerous and scary that Muir dismissed it immediately: a knife-like sliver-bridge of ice 70 feet long.

Not wanting to risk a freezing night on the glacier, Muir realized they had no choice but to try to cross the ice bridge. Just to reach it, they would need to descend a nearly vertical 10-foot wall of ice. If they made it across the bridge, there was still the treacherous climb up the steep far side. The cold, wet weather and failing light made the crossing even more perilous. Muir later said, "Of the many perils encountered in my years of wandering on mountains and glaciers none seemed so plain and stern and merciless as this."

Meanwhile, Stickeen had been trotting along, paying little attention to where they were going. But when they came to the crevasse, he came up and, as Muir told it, "pushed his head past my shoulder, looked down and across, scanned the sliver and its approaches...then looked at me in the face with a startled air of surprise and concern and began to mutter and whine; saying as plainly as if speaking with words, 'Surely, you are not going into that awful place.'

"Never before had the daring midget seemed to know that ice was slippery or that there was any such thing as danger anywhere. His looks and tones of voice when he began to complain and speak his fears were so human that I unconsciously talked to him in sympathy as I would to a frightened boy...'Hush your fears, my boy,' I said, 'we will get across safe, though it is not going to be easy. We must risk our lives to save them.'"

Stickeen, not at all reassured by Muir's brave talk, cried and whined, then with desperate urgency ran off looking for another way. Unsuccessful and defeated, Stickeen returned to watch mournfully as Muir started over the ice bridge.

After nerve-wracking minutes of cutting steps down the ice wall, the whole time balancing over the abyss and hanging on for dear life, Muir straddled the ice and inched his way across the bridge, cutting a narrow flat path for Stickeen to follow. Then, by painstakingly carving steps up the opposite ice-cliff, he slowly made his way up to level ground.

But Stickeen, still too frightened to try even with Muir shouting encouragement, cried "as if howling, 'O-o-oh! What a place! No-o-o, I can never go-o-o down there!'"

Having no other choice, Stickeen finally gathered his courage and peered into the crevasse. He slid his front feet forward and carefully secured them on the first step, then brought his back feet down ever so slowly until all four feet were bunched onto one step, a position that left Stickeen teetering on the sheer ice wall. In this way, Stickeen descended the cliff until he reached the bridge. Bracing himself against the buffeting wind and placing each step with the utmost care, Stickeen made his way across.

Reaching the far cliff face, Stickeen came to the most dangerous part of all. Muir knew that dogs are poor climbers and that if Stickeen were to fall, this would be the place. While Muir desperately tried to think of a way to use his clothing as a rope for hauling Stickeen up, the little dog sat still and seemed to become all eyes and concentration. Intently he observed where and how far apart the steps were. Then in a wild rush Stickeen bounded upward and caught the first step, then the second, the third, fourth, and on and on until he shot up over the cliff to safety.

Stickeen's rescue from deadly peril filled him with a mad release of joy. As Muir described it, Stickeen "flashed and darted hither and thither as if fairly demented, screaming and shouting, swirling round and round in giddy loops and circles like a leaf in a whirlwind, lying down, and rolling over and over...and pouring forth a tumultuous flood of hysterical cries and sobs and gasping mutterings. When I ran up to him, fearing he might die of joy, Stickeen flashed off two or three hundred yards, his feet in a mist of motion; then, turning suddenly, came back in a wild rush and launched himself at my face, almost knocking me down, all the time screeching and screaming and shouting as if saying, 'Saved! saved! saved!'"

Muir told how the ice-bridge crossing affected his little friend: "Thereafter Stickeen was a changed dog. During the rest of the trip, instead of holding aloof, he always lay by my side, and tried to keep me constantly in sight.... At night, when all was quiet about the campfire, he would come to me and rest his head on my knee...and as he caught my eye he seemed to be trying to say, 'Wasn't that an awful time we had together on the glacier?'"

Muir always finished the story of Stickeen by telling his listeners how much the episode had taught him. "At first the least promising and least known of my dog-friends, he suddenly became the best known of them all. In that dreadful crevasse...I saw through him down into the depths of our common nature. Our storm-battle for life brought him to light, and through him as through a window I have ever since been looking with deeper sympathy into all my fellow mortals."*

Take a few moments now to think about your experiences with animals. Have you ever had a chance to see some unexpected quality in an animal? Perhaps it was bravery like Stickeen's, or kindness, or loyalty, or any other special trait. Describe what it was like:

_____

_____

_____

_____

_____

_____

_____

_____

_____

_____

_____

_____

*If you would like to know more about Stickeen and his wilderness adventures, you can read the book **Stickeen**, by John Muir. The publisher is Heyday Books, PO Box 9145, Berkeley, California 94709 USA

Interview
with Nature

"Did you know that trees talk? Well they do. They talk to each other, and they'll talk to you if you listen....I have learned a lot from trees: sometimes about the weather, sometimes about animals, sometimes about the Great Spirit."

–Walking Buffalo, Stoney Indian, Canada

John Muir said Stickeen "enlarged my life, extended its boundaries." Getting to know the lives of other things can broaden and enrich your own life.

In this activity, you'll choose a rock, plant, or animal from your site that you feel has an interesting story to tell. Treat your choice as a "friend" who is sharing life with you on Planet Earth.

In your interview, try to see life from this new point of view, as you write answers to a series of questions. You can use your imagination to come up with the answers, and if you like, you can try to listen quietly for thoughts that tell you how your friend might respond.

Now, select your rock, plant or animal. Get to know it as well as you can. If possible, look at it from different angles. For example, with a rock or plant, you could feel its texture with your hands. See if anything grows on it. Look for evidence that something might have harmed or affected it in some way, such as fire, drought, erosion, and so on. Stand a short distance away and see how it fits in and interacts with its surroundings.

I was at the primate exhibit at the National Zoo in Washington, D.C. some years ago, watching an old, dignified gorilla leaning against the glass wall of his cage. He was just inches away from the crowd of visitors, some of whom were teasing him by jumping up and down like monkeys.

Ignoring the people, the gorilla gazed off into the distance, his mind somewhere else. You could see that he seemed very alert and intelligent. Watching him, I wondered if he was remembering his free days as a young gorilla in Africa. As I watched the gorilla and the people acting like monkeys, I thought, "Who has the most dignity?"

In Western countries especially, many people think of animals as unintelligent, lower creatures. Because of these thoughts, some people justify treating animals cruelly. But the secret of developing close relationships with them is to avoid thinking of them as inferiors. When you treat animals with respect, they become less wary and reveal more of themselves to you.

Interview with Nature

Choose one of the following categories and answer the questions that seem most interesting to you. Remember that the questions are there only to give you ideas. Feel free, if you prefer, to make up your own questions and conversations.

Rock

Though we don't think of rocks as being aware of what happens around them, yet like everything else, rocks uniquely influence and interact with the environment. Find a special rock. If it's big enough, climb up on it and find a comfortable place to sit. If you choose a smaller rock, hold it in your hands and look at it. Try to feel what it's like to be a rock.

How old are you?
Have you always been the size you are now?
Where did you come from?
What is it like living in this particular place?
Who comes to visit you?
What events have you seen in your life?
Is there something special you would like to tell me?"

Geologists say that some rocks in the Grand Canyon are 2 billion years old. It's fun to think of all the things that have happened to those rocks since they were created. Mountain ranges have formed and been worn down, deserts have come and gone, and seas have arrived and departed. Dinosaurs, mammoths, and camels have all in their turn walked the land.

Plant

Find a special plant. It can be a tree that's big enough to climb, or it could be a very small and delicate plant, like a tiny wildflower. Try to see the world from the plant's point of view. Ask your plant the same questions given for a rock.

Animal

Look for an animal that is easy to observe. It might be a bird, fish, insect, or lizard. As carefully as you can, follow it wherever it goes. Imagine yourself becoming the animal. Try not to disturb it or frighten it.

Where are you going?
What are you trying to accomplish?
Are there any predators that you need to watch out for?
What do you eat, and how do you find your food?
Where do you live? Alone or with others?
Do you ever travel to other places?
What would you like to tell others about yourself?

Write your interview:

"If you love it enough, anything will talk to you."

–George Washington Carver

Can you think of something special you can do for your rock, plant or animal?

"Human and animal love, hope, and fear are essentially the same, derived from the same source and fall on all alike like sunshine."

–John Muir

Living in

In the American Southwest many desert travelers, on arriving at a spring, would drink and replenish their water supplies. Then they would deliberately set up camp a short distance away in order to assure that the desert animals would have clear access to their only source of water.

Wild animals and plants bring joy to our lives. By considering their needs, we can ensure their continued survival. Before we do anything in nature, it's important to ask, "How does this affect the animals and plants that live here?" It often takes only a little more effort on our part to protect their needs.

Harmony with Nature

Think about your site and how it would be affected if someone decided to use the area for a campsite, house, or road. What are some things you could suggest to the builders to help protect the plants and animals? (For example, you might suggest that they use only those places where the soil can take heavy traffic.) Tell where you would place the road, cabin, etc., and how big it should be.

We can learn about living in harmony with nature from many traditional cultures. Paul Brand was an American boy who grew up in the mountains of South India in the 1920's. Life for the people in his village was very simple. There were no stores, electricity, or even roads. Rice was their most important food, and they grew everything they ate.

When rice begins to grow, it must be covered with water. To keep the water in place, the villagers built many small dams and levees along the hillsides. Because the ground was steep in the village where Paul Brand lived, the water would flow out over the levees of one field and down into the next one until it reached the lowest level.

In the following story, Paul Brand shares a lesson he learned about the importance of caring for the earth and its resources.

"One day I was playing in the mud of a rice field with a half-dozen other little boys. We were catching frogs, racing to see who would be the first to get three. It was a wonderful way to get dirty from head to foot in the shortest possible time. But suddenly we were all scrambling to get out of the paddy.

"One of the boys had spotted an old man walking across the path toward us. We all knew him and called him 'Tata,' meaning 'grandpa.' He was the keeper of the dams. He walked slowly, stooped over a bit, as though he were always looking at the ground. Old age is very much respected in India, and we boys shuffled our feet and waited in silence for what we knew was going to be a [scolding].

"He came over to us and asked what we were doing. 'Catching frogs,' we answered. He stared down at the churned-up mud and flattened young rice plants in the corner where we had been playing, and I was expecting him to talk about the rice seedlings that we

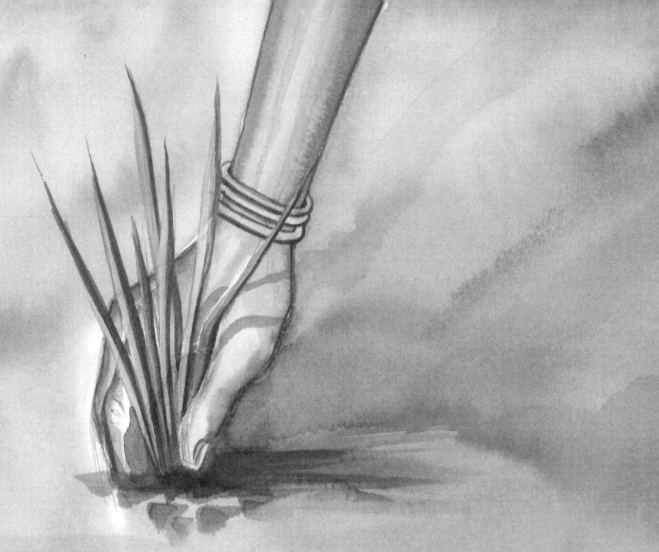

had spoiled. Instead, he bent down and scooped up a handful of mud. 'What is this?' he asked.

"The biggest boy among us took the responsibility of answering for all of us. 'It's mud, Tata.'

"'Whose mud is it?' the old man asked.

"'It's your mud, Tata. This is your field.'

"Then the old man turned and looked across the dam. 'What do you see there in that channel?' he asked.

"'That is water running over into the lower field,' the biggest boy answered.

"For the first time Tata looked angry. 'Come with me and I will show you water.'

"We followed him a few steps along the dam, and he pointed to the next channel, where clear water was running. 'That is what water looks like,' he said. Then he led us back to our nearest channel and said, 'Is that water?'

"We hung our heads. 'No, Tata, that is mud—muddy water,' the oldest boy answered. He had heard all this before and did not want to prolong the question-and-answer session, so he hurried on. 'And the mud from your field is being carried away to the field below, and it will never come back, because mud always runs downhill, never up

again. We are sorry, Tata, and we will never do this again.'

"But Tata was not ready to stop his lesson as quickly as that, so he went on to tell us that just one handful of mud would grow enough rice for one meal for one person, and it would do it twice every year for years and years into the future.

"'That mud flowing over the dam has given my family food every year from long before I was born, and before my grandfather was born. It would have given my grandchildren food, and then given their grandchildren food forever. Now it will never feed us again. When you see mud in the channels of water, you know that life is flowing away from the mountains.'

"The old man walked slowly back across the path, pausing a moment to adjust with his foot the grass clod in our muddy channel so that no more water flowed through it. We were silent and uncomfortable as we went off to find some other place to play. I had gotten a dose of traditional Indian folk education that would remain with me as long as I lived. Soil was life, and every generation was responsible for preserving it for future generations..."

Caring for Your Site

Here are some projects that will help you care for your site. Choose one that meets the special needs of your area, and that you might enjoy doing. Your guide can help you decide on a good choice.

Before you begin a project, think about it from the point of view of the plants and animals. Will it help them? In one traditional culture, the leaders would carefully consider how any important action would affect the people living in the village seven generations later!

Soil Conservation Projects

As Paul Brand's story shows, one of the best ways to care for a site is by protecting the soil from erosion. The plants benefit, and because animals depend on plants for food and shelter, they benefit, too.

See if you can find any places in your site where the life-giving soil is washing away. Look for signs of water running down a steep trail or road, or across bare ground such as might occur at overused campsites.

The upper layer of soil and leaves softens the rain's impact and prevents erosion. The topsoil absorbs water like a sponge, and holds food for trees and other plants. When people remove the topsoil, the ground loses its protection against the elements, and the raindrops beat on it like tiny hammers. On sloping ground, the rain can carry away huge amounts of soil. The following projects help preserve the topsoil.

WATER BARS. In an area where water runs rapidly downhill, you can place logs across its path. As water travels downhill, it picks up speed and carries away more soil. Placing logs at intervals along the slope slows the water's progress and prevents soil erosion.

For each log, dig a diagonal trench across the water's path. Make the trench deep enough so that just two inches of the log stick up above the ground. Make sure the logs are long enough to prevent the water from flowing around them. The logs should also divert the water to an area at the side of the channel where it can be safely absorbed into the ground.

To anchor each log, drive stakes into the ground at each end on the downhill side. (You can also drive stakes on the uphill side, if you think they'll help hold the log firmly in place.) Pound the tops of the stakes down level with the tops of the logs so people won't trip on them.

MULCHING. If your site has areas of bare dirt or abandoned roads, you can reclaim the soil by mulching. Gather leaves, wood chips, lawn clippings and other natural materials and spread them over the ground in a layer 1-2 inches thick. Mulch protects the soil, absorbs water, and provides food for plants.

Keep the mulch away from tree trunks so that creatures that live in the soil won't damage the bark. If there's a fairly steep slope uphill from where you're working, you may need to build water bars (see above) to keep the mulch from being washed away.

WILLOW STAKES. Did you know that if you plant a willow branch in the ground, it will sprout and grow into a new tree? You can start other river trees such as cottonwoods and poplars the same way.

If there's a stream in your area, you can plant willow stakes along the banks to help stabilize the soil and prevent erosion. The trees help keep the water cool and provide shelter for wildlife.

The best time to plant willow stakes is from late fall to early spring, since the trees are dormant at this time. Cut a stake from a willow branch at least a half-inch thick and at least 18 inches long, so that the planted end will reach down through the dry topsoil to where the soil is wet all year.

After sawing off a suitable branch, shape the thicker end (the one toward the trunk) into a point with an axe. At the other end, make a straight, flat cut.

If the ground is hard and rocky, you may need to dig a hole first. If the soil is wet and soft, hammer the pointed end of the stake into the ground. To prevent the tops from splitting, put a board over the flat end of the stake as you pound.

Remember to plant each stake deep enough to reach wet soil, to prevent it from drying out in hot weather. Also, make sure

that one-half to two-thirds of the stake is buried. This helps the tree grow a root system that's big enough to support the tree.

You should see noticeable growth within one year. The trees you plant will soon make a big difference to the health of the stream and to everything that lives there.

Habitat Preservation Projects

PROTECTING SENSITIVE AREAS. Human traffic can harm delicate areas such as small wetlands, meadows filled with wildflowers, and groves of old trees. You can help protect these fragile areas by laying out a trail that lets people enjoy the site from a safe distance. You may also need to block off older trails that lead into the area.

NATURAL AREAS. This project demonstrates what happens when nature takes back land after humans have managed it. It works best in urban areas that have lawns and gardens.

Find a suitable area, like a lawn or pasture, and ask for permission to use the site. Then mark off the site with a boundary. The area should be at least 400 square feet (20' wide by 20' long). You can use a smaller site if you have to. Build a simple "fence" with string and stakes. Make a sign that explains what you're doing. For example: "This area is being reclaimed for nature study." Your plot may begin to look wild and neglected, and the sign will prevent people from "improving" it by mowing the weeds.

Before long, you'll see wild plants begin to take back the area. To help nature along, try growing some native plant species. Ask for them at a local nursery. As time passes, nature will create a wild garden at your site, complete with insects, birds, and small mammals.

These are only a few of the many conservation projects you can do at your site. For example, you could also build nesting boxes for birds or bats, remove barbed wire from trees, and pick up litter. For more ideas, read Malcolm Margolin's delightful book, *The Earth Manual* (available for $14.95, postpaid, from Heyday Books, PO Box 9145, Berkeley, California, 94709 USA). Many of the guidelines for the projects described here were adapted from that book.

Write down the project(s) you'd like to try, and what you hope to accomplish.

Letting Others Know

This true story tells how a nine-year-old girl named Alison convinced a stranger to protect something that was very important to her.

In the forest near her home in California, there was a very special tree that Alison loved. She called it "The Giving Tree" because it gave her happiness. One day, Alison heard that some trees in the forest would soon be cut down. She ran into the forest to check on her tree, which was a stately, 140-foot sugar pine. Just as she feared, she found a thin blue line painted on the tree's bark that meant: "Take this one."

Alison went to the forest owner's house and asked him to save the tree. The owner, who was a land developer, explained that a tree of that size was worth $7,000. He hadn't seen the tree but told Alison that another one would someday grow to take its place.

Alison knew her tree was over a hundred years old, and she felt that a hundred years was too long to wait. So she offered to buy the tree, thinking that her friends at school could help her. The owner said no, he couldn't let Alison buy the tree. But before Alison left, she got the owner to promise he wouldn't let the tree be cut down until he had a chance to see it the next day.

At five o'clock in the morning, Alison went to her tree to keep it from being chopped down before the owner came. When the owner finally arrived and saw the tree, he was impressed by its tremendous size and felt that it was indeed very special. Knowing there were very few sugar pines that large and so close to town, he decided to save "The Giving Tree" so that people could continue to enjoy it.

Think about your area. Which part is most special to you? It could be an uplifting view, a grove of trees, or a type of wildflower that you've never seen before. In the space below, describe it in detail. Later, you'll share this description with a friend who will try to find it.

An Example of Letting Others Know

I was hiking around Eagle Lake near Lake Tahoe, California, when a friend said, "See if you can find the rock that looks like a bear." I found myself looking carefully at every boulder we passed until I finally found the rock that indeed looked remarkably like a bear.

Here is the description I wrote to share Bear Rock with other friends: *When you arrive and first see Eagle Lake, go left onto the lakeside trail. In a few minutes you'll come to a pair of small boulders on your right. Go a few feet past the first one, then look back. What kind of animal does the rock on the right resemble? Besides a bear, others have said it looks like a frog or a beaver. What does it look like to you?*

Sharing Your Site with a Friend

John Muir had great love for Yosemite Valley in the Sierra Nevada mountains of California. Yosemite is one of the most beautiful and awesome places on earth, with waterfalls that drop hundreds of feet over granite cliffs into a glacier-carved valley. But for Muir, it wasn't enough just to enjoy this special place by himself. He longed to share its treasures with others.

In the spring of 1903, Muir had a chance to show Yosemite to Theodore Roosevelt, the newly-elected president of the United States. During a three-day visit, John took his new friend "Teddy" on a camping trip during which they slept under 2500-year-old giant sequoia redwood trees. These enormous trees reach heights of 300 feet and are so thick that it takes 15 grown men to form a ring around them with outstretched arms.

The spectacular views and the quiet of the mountains, along with experiences like being covered with snow while they slept, fired Teddy Roosevelt's love of nature and fused a lifelong friendship with John Muir. Their long talks by the campfire's glow inspired the President to create national forests to protect 148 million acres of wildland. Thus John's beloved Yosemite and many other magnificent areas were preserved for the enjoyment of future generations.

It's your turn now to share nature's beauty with a friend by showing him or her the unique features of your site. Think back to the first time you visited the area. Which places caught your attention? What experiences helped you to appreciate your site? In addition to leading your friend around and sharing the many interesting places, you can include some of these simple activities.

You might begin by seeing if your friend can find the place you described in the *Letting Others Know* activity and the "best view" you sketched in the *Adventure Hunt* during Visit One. You could also share the poem you wrote during Visit Three and tell how your conservation project will benefit the animals and plants that live at your site.

Look for ways to create a sense of excitement and discovery. For example, to share a pond filled with frogs, stop before you reach the water and ask your friend to listen for a "special clue." Or, to point out an active birds' nest, creep up as close as possible without scaring the birds, then ask your friend to look for something special nearby. It will add to the excitement if you can both keep silent while the search is going on.

I once took some friends to see the Grand Canyon for the first time. This amazing canyon is more than a mile deep and 280 miles long. I put blindfolds over my friends' eyes and led them to the railing. When I took off the blindfolds, the view left them stunned. For a long time they stood in silence, absorbed in the canyon's beauty.

Just for fun, send an invitation card to someone you think would enjoy your special place. Your invitation might look something like this:

Bringing a Friend

You are invited:
to explore
the Giant Forest
Your Guide is: José

Things I want to do.

Write the special places and activities you would like to share with your guest.

Here are two more activities. Feel free to think of other ways to share your place.

Meet a Tree

Do you have a favorite tree in your site? You can introduce your guest to it with this game. (If there aren't any trees, you can play Meet a Place.)

First, make sure there aren't things like poisonous vines or ants living on the tree.

Then, before your friend sees the tree, put a blindfold over his or her eyes. (Closed eyes work, too, but a blindfold is more fun.)

Hold your friend's elbow and hand and carefully walk toward the tree you've chosen. Make sure you avoid such things as overhanging branches, rocks, logs, holes and poisonous plants. (Remember: you are the eyes for both of you!)

Speak only when it's necessary—to get around obstacles, for example. Keeping silent helps your friend hear the sounds of nature and get a feel for the land.

Give your friend a few minutes to explore the tree by touch, sound, and smell before leading the way back to the starting place.

Take off the blindfold and ask your friend to find the tree.

Animal Riddle

Choose an animal that lives at your site.

In the spaces below, write down six clues about the animal. Put the clues in order, with the hardest first and the easiest last. Make the last clue so obvious that it's easy to guess the animal. (To get ideas for clues, see *All Our Relations* in Visit Two, or look at a field guide to local animals.)

Read the clues aloud, one at a time, and see if your friend can guess the animal.

Here is a sample game. Take a piece of paper and cover everything except the first clue. After you read each line, try to guess the answer. Continue down the page until you've gone through all the clues. Check your final guess against the coded answer at the bottom of the page. To solve the code, replace each letter in the code with the next letter in the alphabet. Example: A Z S = B A T

1. When I walk I move my two right legs, then my two left legs.
2. I eat early in the morning and late at night.
3. I have four or five babies during the 50-60 years of my life.
4. I live in forest and grassland and eat plants.
5. I take mud baths to protect my skin from sun and insects.
6. I weigh up to seven tons and have big ears. I live in Africa and use my long nose to gather food and drink water.

D K D O G Z M S

— — — — — — — —

My Animal Riddle

Clue #1 _____

Clue #2 _____

Clue #3 _____

Clue #4 _____

Clue #5 _____

Clue #6 _____

5

Fifth Visit
An Inspirational Evening and Morning

he evening is a wonderful time to be outdoors. Many animals are active and easily seen. The day's last light gives everything a rich, golden color that some call "glory light," and the western sky fills with great beauty. Then, as our sun leaves us, we see other stars—just a few at first, then thousands.

On this visit, you'll witness the magical, calm beauty of evening and morning. Because each sunset and sunrise is a unique surprise, you can never tell what exciting things you'll see.

I recently saw five swans resting on a large pond at the Sacramento Wildlife Refuge in northern California. Sundown was not far off, so I stayed to see if the swans would fly off the water. Instead, hundreds of swans flew in from every direction and landed on the pond. I realized I'd discovered the swans' gathering place.

As the sky turned violet over California's Coast Range, flock after flock gracefully fell from the sky. Slowing their descent with outstretched wings, the swans seemed suspended in the air as they drifted downward.

Long after the sun set and the scene disappeared in total blackness, I continued to hear the splashing and *"woo-ho, woo-woo, woo-ho"* of arriving flocks.

All over the world, many wonderful events happen at sunset and sunrise. Discover the "special events" at those times in your area. Use the following section, *Getting Ready for the Night*, to prepare for your visit.

the Heart of Nature

If possible, go on an evening when the sky is clear enough to see the sunset and stars.

This session is presented as a solo overnight experience, but it can also be done as follows:

1) Ask an adult guide to camp nearby, where he or she can be close if you need help.

2) Ask an adult to share your campsite.

3) Visit the site in the evening and do the first activities, then return at dawn and finish the visit.

Discuss your plans with your parents and guide, and give them a time when you expect to return.

If you'll be going a distance from home or camp, you may also want to bring the following: whistle, compass, map, and signaling mirror.

If you dress in dark-colored clothing, the nighttime animals won't be able to see you as well. And they'll be less able to detect the light from your flashlight if you put red plastic or red cellophane over the lens.

Arrive at your site at least two hours before sunset so you'll have plenty of time to set up camp, have a last walk around, and find a place nearby where you can see the sunset. You'll want to be at your sunset viewpoint 15 minutes before actual sundown. If there isn't a place with a view of the sunset, find an area where you can see the open sky. Lakes and ponds work well, too, if there isn't an open area nearby.

Getting Ready for the Night

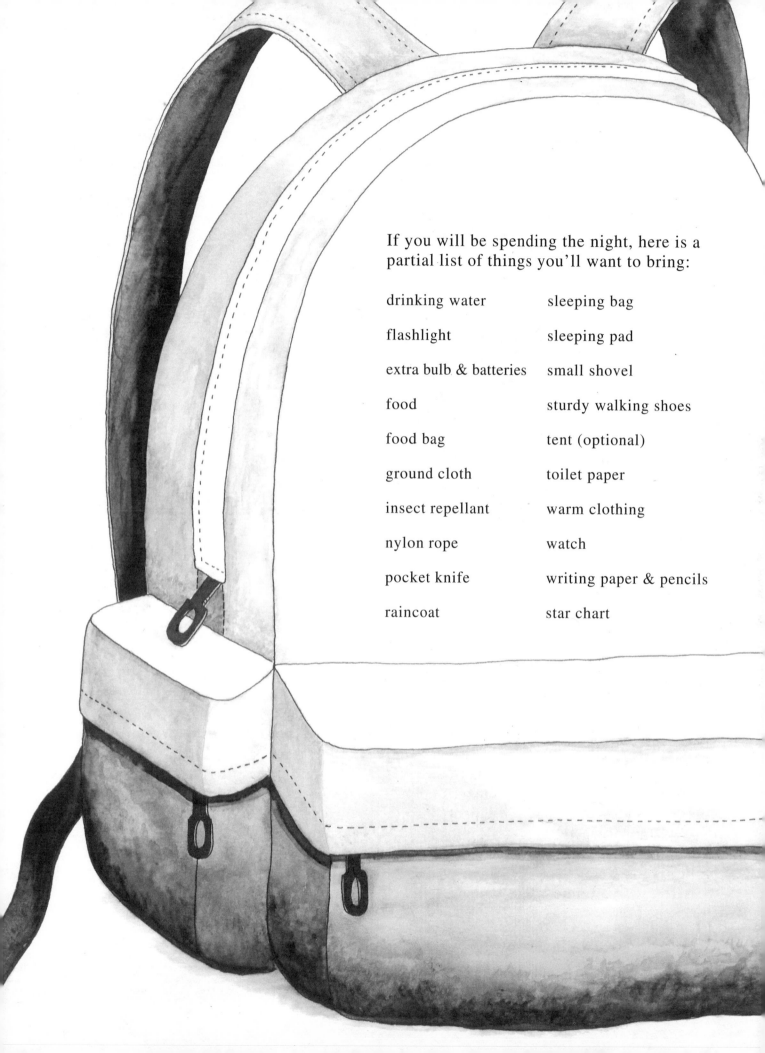

If you will be spending the night, here is a partial list of things you'll want to bring:

drinking water	sleeping bag
flashlight	sleeping pad
extra bulb & batteries	small shovel
food	sturdy walking shoes
food bag	tent (optional)
ground cloth	toilet paper
insect repellant	warm clothing
nylon rope	watch
pocket knife	writing paper & pencils
raincoat	star chart

Selecting & Setting Up Camp

Look for a camping place close to your sunset viewing area. It'll be dark when you're finished, so you'll want to set up camp within easy walking distance.

Choose a site where the soil is dry and well drained. This will help you avoid mosquitoes and minimize your impact. Stay at least 200 feet away from a stream or lake, to reduce the chance of polluting the water.

After you've found a likely place, look around to make sure it's safe. Some areas to avoid include: Places where there are dead trees or branches overhead, cliffs where rocks might fall on your campsite, dry stream beds that can experience dangerous flash floods, the nests of ants and bees, poisonous plants, and high ground that is exposed to lightning or stormy weather.

To keep animals from disturbing your sleep, hang your food from a tree, well away from the campsite.

Going For a Walk

"(Nature) is never the same, even from day to day, or even from hour to hour."
— Clarence Dutton, geologist

After setting up camp, go for a walk around your site and visit some of your favorite places. These might include the place where you sketched your best view, wrote a poem, built a conservation project, interviewed something in nature, or saw a special animal.

Enjoy these places and see how each has changed since your first visit. Does the area look different at this time of day and this part of the season? Some things you might notice are new kinds of flowers, animals that have moved away from the site, different water levels in streams or ponds, and leaves growing larger or turning color.

Write down a few of the changes you've noticed.

Sunset Watch

Arrive 15 minutes before sunset and bring a flashlight and warm clothing.

This activity helps you notice and enjoy the exciting events that happen around sunset. On the next two pages you'll find a list of things you might observe. What you see will depend on the area and time of year. Mark each event in the order it happens. For example, if you first notice that the day birds are quiet, you would write number "1" next to *day birds*. If you hear an owl or other night bird a little later, write number "2" for *owl calling*, and so on. If an event is continually changing, like the clouds turning color, you can note the changes by writing more than one number for the event—for example, "5" and "8" *clouds change color.*

Besides watching the sun set in the western sky, look in all the other directions. Don't worry about missing something or getting the order exactly as things happen. Just put a number by the things you see when you see them. Remember, the most important part is to enjoy the sunset. Looking for the events in the list will help you do this.

Because each location is unique, you'll probably see other events as well. You might see a flock of birds gathering in a tree, for example, or a mammal beginning its evening ramble, fish jumping for flying insects, or frogs singing. When you see anything special, write it down under *other events*. Write a number for each of these events so you have a record of when it occurred.

If your camp is hard to find or a good distance away, be sure there's plenty of light to walk back to the campsite. Even if you carry a flashlight, some trails are best walked before total darkness, because of overhanging branches or the presence of snakes. You may need to leave before the first star appears. As you walk back, continue to look for and record events.

If your camp is close by, or the trail is wide and well marked and easy to follow, you'll probably want to stay and watch the night sky as it fills with stars.

Sunset Watch

Location:_____ Date:_____

__ First planet or star

__ Long shadows

__ Bats fly

__ Everything to the east is lit by glory light.

__ Things far to the west lose their day color.

__ Day birds quiet

__ Hills turn color (describe) _____

_____

__ Sky is dark except to the west

__ Owl or other night bird calling or flying

__ Campfire or lights of car or building become visible

__ Clouds change color (describe) _____

_____

__ Sun falls below the horizon

__ Individual shadows blend together (where you are)

__ Night insects active

__ Night shadow completely covers hills to the east

__ Sky turns a soft pink or violet color (after sundown)

__ Moon appears or brightens

__ Clouds no longer visible

__ North Star and Little Dipper or Southern Cross appear

__ Temperature cools

__ Wind speed or direction changes

__ First shooting star or meteor

Other Events: Record and number any other events you noticed—for example, perhaps you saw a satellite or heard a wolf or coyote.

Celebrating the Night

Sunset and twilight are special times. Think of how the day turning to night affects you and your site. Try to capture the essence of what has happened by writing a Haiku or Vertical Poem (see Visit Three), or any other form of written expression.

"When alone at night in the depths of these woods, the stillness is...sublime. Every leaf seems to speak. One gets close to Nature and the love of beauty grows as it cannot in the distractions of a camp."

–John Muir

If this is your first night staying outdoors alone, it's normal to feel a little uncomfortable, or even fearful of the dark. From your past visits, you know much more about the things around you than you did at first. From your talks with your guide, you should have an idea of which wild animals in your area you don't have to worry about.

A good way to stay calm and brave is by not allowing your imagination to excite you. When people hear a sound in the night, they sometimes imagine all kinds of scary things and begin to fear the worst. Remember that small animals often make lots of noise that makes them seem bigger than they are. (Whenever you are bothered by an unknown noise, try speaking loudly or whistling to see if the sound stops.)

There's a story about some older children who were teasing a young girl about a ghost that lived in a dark part of the house. The girl immediately got up and went to the "haunted" spot. Not finding any ghost, she returned to the others and expressed her disappointment. Seeing her bravery, the older children never teased her again.

Like the girl, if you look fear in the face, it will cease to bother you. If there is something that frightens you, try walking over to it to see what it is, so that your mind will be at ease.

A 10-year-old friend of mine was spending his first night out alone when he noticed a mysterious shape in the distance. After a long time of anxiously wondering what it was, he remembered the story of the girl and marched right up to the white glow and looked at it with his flashlight. To his relief, he saw that it was only a tree stump! He laughed and was finally able to get to sleep.

Welcoming the Night

(and overcoming fears)

Would you believe that most of us can see better than a bear at night, and almost as well as a cat? Our night vision seldom reaches full power, because we're usually surrounded by artificial light. It takes our eyes 45 minutes to recover their full night vision after looking into strong light.

You'll need to use your flashlight to see where you're going and to read this book, of course. But sometime during the night, try turning off your flashlight for an hour or so, and see how your night vision improves.

Exploring the

The following account was written by a wilderness explorer who lived "with the stars in the open...night after night" during a seven-month journey. 🟊 In 1887, Sir Francis Younghusband, then a young British military officer, was asked by his superiors to go on a mission of vital importance for his country. To fulfill his assignment, he was required to travel from Beijing, China to India by way of the Gobi Desert and the Himalaya mountains. 🟊 Since he did not share a common language with his guides, he spent day after day essentially alone in the silent wilderness. He commented, "[The stillness] was so profound that, when at the end of many weeks I arrived at a patch of grass and trees, the twittering of the birds and the whir of insects sounded like the roar of a London Street." It was a daring and dangerous journey for the first European to successfully cross the world's largest desert and highest mountain range, but for him there was an even more important discovery, which he described as follows: 🟊 "To enable my eight camels to feed by daylight, I used to start at five o'clock in the afternoon and march till one or two in the morning.... The sunset glow would fade away. Star after star would spring into sight till the whole vault of heaven was glistening with diamond points of light. Above me and all round me stars were shining out of the deep sapphire sky...and a great stillness would be over all.... 🟊 In this unbroken stillness and with the eye free to rove all round with nothing in any direction to stay its vision, and being as I was many weeks' distance from any settled human habitation, I often had the feeling of being more connected with the starry firmament than with this Earth.... 🟊 I knew also that the number of stars, besides those few thousands which I saw, had to be numbered in hundreds of millions. All this was astonishing, and the knowledge of it filled me with wonder at the immensity of the Starry Universe. But it was not the

Heart of Nature

mere magnitude of this world that impressed me. What stirred me was the Presence, subtly felt, of some mighty all-pervading Influence which ordered the courses of the heavenly hosts and permeated every particle. ❧ We cannot watch the sun go down day after day, and after it has set see the stars appear, rise to the meridian and disappear below the opposite horizon in regular procession, without being impressed by the order which prevails. We feel that the whole is kept together in punctual fashion, and is not mere chaos and chance. The presence of some Power upholding, sustaining, and directing the whole is deeply impressed upon us. And in this Presence so steadfast, so calm, so constant, we feel soothed and steadied. Deep peace and satisfaction fill our souls." ❧ When you're alone outdoors, especially at night, you'll have wonderful opportunities to explore the mystery of Life and your relationship to the universe. Another account by Sir Francis Younghusband is helpful. This one tells about a visit to Tibet: ❧ "After arrival in camp I went off into the mountains alone. It was a heavenly evening. The sun was flooding the mountain slopes with slanting light. Calm and deep peace lay over the valley below me—I seemed in tune with all the world, and all the world seemed in tune with me. ❧ After the high tension of the last 15 months, I was free to let my soul relax. So I let it open itself out without restraint. And in its sensitive state it was receptive of the finest impressions and quickly responsive to every call. I seemed to be truly in harmony with the Heart of Nature. ❧ And my experience was this—I had a curious sense of being literally in love with the world. I felt as if I could hardly contain myself for the love which was bursting within me. It seemed to me as if the world itself were nothing but love. ❧ My experience was no unique experience. It was an experience the like of which has come to many men and women in every land in all ages. It may not be common; but it is not unusual."

Many people have shared the profound awe of the night that Sir Francis Younghusband felt. This evening, you'll have a chance to explore the Heart of Nature for yourself.

Go to a clear area where you can see the open sky. Lie down, relax, and let your mind roam among the distant stars...

How far out does this universe reach? What's it like beyond the farthest star? How long has the universe existed? What is it that keeps the sun and earth in their orbits?

Think about how you and your special place are influenced by these vast forces of the universe. For example, what would it be like if the sun were twice as far away, or if there were only half as much rain?

In what other ways are you connected to all that you see around you?

On a clear, dark night you're likely to see about two thousand stars—out of the one billion billion stars that are known to exist.

Light travels at 186,000 miles a second. Yet some stars are so far away that it takes hundreds, thousands, or even millions of years for their light to reach us. When you look at a star, you may be seeing light that began its long journey hundreds of years ago.

Because the earth rotates, it's always sunrise somewhere in the world. During the night you travel toward another meeting with the sun at a speed of hundreds of miles per hour. You can experience the earth's spin if you watch the night sky and see how stars rise over the horizon in the east and set in the west. Notice the positions of particular stars or constellations. If you wake up during the night, you can track their progress across the sky.

You'll see some of the stars moving in a circle around Polaris, the North Star, if you live in the northern hemisphere, or around true south if you live in the southern hemisphere.

N
W + E
S

If you are sleepy, go ahead and rest for the night. You watched the sun go down, so why not try to wake up early enough to greet the sun's return. Then start reading the Journey's End section on the next page.

"The time to hear bird music is between four and six in the morning. Seven o'clock is not too late, but by eight the fine rapture is over..."

–Donald Culross Peattie, *An Almanac for Moderns*

What do you feel while you gaze at the night sky? Like Sir Francis Younghusband, take time to describe what your experience has been like this evening.

Good morning! Is it still dark? Can you still see planets and stars? Have the birds started singing? Can you see any sign of the approaching sun?

Dawn, with its fresh golden light, is a wonderful time to be outdoors. Listen for animals waking up. See the sunlight flowing into the trees. Watch as our own star climbs higher and beams its warmth on the land.

Welcome the sun's return and the life it gives to all. Enjoy the sunrise for as long as you like.

If you're still sleepy, try splashing cold water on your face to wake up. Because this morning's activities will take about an hour, you might like to eat something first. When you're ready, go to a favorite place and read the following story.

Journey's End

The Man Who Planted
Hope and Grew Happiness

This story is about a land that was dying, and the man who brought it back to life. It's a modern-day legend based on Jean Giono's childhood experiences with his father.

In 1910, Elzeard Bouffier moved to the ancient part of France where the Alps thrust down into Provence. The land then was desolate, and the villages mostly abandoned. The wind blew harshly and water was scarce. The entire region was almost a desert. It was a hard land, and only a few hard, embittered souls remained to scratch out their living from the barren soil, and they treated each other as cruelly as the land treated them.

Elzeard had once had a farm in the lowlands, but after his only son died, followed soon after by his wife, he had withdrawn at the age of 52 to seek solitude as a shepherd, living alone with his lambs and his dog.

Elzeard could see that the land was dying for lack of trees. Years ago, fuel gatherers had burned most of the trees for charcoal. Having no pressing business of his own, he decided to do what he could to help the land.

Each day as he followed his sheep along the mountain slopes, Elzeard would gather acorns in a woolen sack. When he returned at evening to the stone house he had restored, he poured out the acorns on his wooden table. In the soft glow of his lantern he inspected each of them, choosing only the most perfect ones. When he had selected 100 acorns, he retired for the night.

The next day as he walked, Elzeard used an iron staff to make small holes in the ground. In each hole he placed one of his acorns. Once he was asked if the land belonged to him. He answered no. Did he know whose property it was? He did not. He supposed it was community land, or perhaps belonged to people who cared nothing about it. He was not interested in finding out whose it was, and continued to plant his 100 acorns every day with the greatest care.

After three years, his acorns had grown to be healthy young oak trees. Where before nothing had been growing, there now stood a small but thriving forest.

World War I came and went, and through it all Elzeard continued planting his acorns, adding some beech trees and birches in the valleys. When the war ended, his first trees, now 10 years old and taller than a man, covered the surrounding hillsides like a vibrant green carpet. The forest they made was 3 kilometers wide and four times as long.

A chain reaction had started, and the first signs of life began to return to the land. Water was seen flowing in brooks that had been dry for as long as the people could remember.

The wind had scattered seeds, and with the return of the water, there reappeared willows, rushes, meadows, and flowers.

The transformation took place so gradually that it caused little notice. People thought the sudden growth of little trees was due to some whim of nature. Thus, no one meddled with his work. If he had been detected, there would have been opposition.

In 1933, he received a visit from a government ranger who warned him against lighting outdoor fires so as to protect the "natural" forest that was growing in that area. Elzeard assured the man that he would be careful and would do everything he could to protect the trees.

A few years later a whole delegation arrived to examine this new forest. It was impossible not to be captivated by the beauty of those young trees, now 20-25 feet tall. In order to keep people from harming the trees, the chief government official placed the whole area under the protection of the state.

And what of Elzeard himself? Regular toil in the vigorous mountain air, simple living, and a peaceful spirit had made him into one of God's athletes. At the age of 76 he was still going strong. He ignored the second World War just as he had the first. When it was over, people returning through the area were entranced by the scenery. Everything was changed, even the air. Where once harsh, dry winds had blown, there were now gentle breezes laden with scents. The soothing sound that floated down from the mountains came from the young trees. And water was plentiful.

Many stayed to rebuild the villages. New families were started, and the spirit of youth, laughter, and hope returned to the region. Where 40 years before there had been only a few desperate people, over 10,000 now owed their happiness to the efforts of one man. Through patience and perseverance, Elzeard had brought a dying land back to life. In 1947 he died peacefully at the age of 87.*

*See *Sharing the Joy of Nature*, by Dawn Publications, if you would like to read the complete story of *The Man Who Planted Hope and Grew Happiness*.

Your visits have probably helped you feel a sense of caring much like Elzeard Bouffier's. In the years ahead, perhaps you, too, will have an opportunity to preserve the beauty of a special place in nature.

Each of us can act to make the earth a better place, and by doing so, we help it remain a beautiful place to live. It may seem sometimes that just one person can do very little. But when we each do our part, it *does* help, as the following stories prove.

While walking on a beach one morning, a woman discovered thousands of starfish scattered over the sand, thrown out of the ocean by the previous night's storm. Knowing the starfish would die if she didn't help, the woman began carrying them back to the sea.

Another beach walker, watching the woman and seeing that she could save only a few out of the thousands that were strewn all over the beach, said, "You can't save *all* the starfish. It's hopeless — so why bother?"

The woman looked at the man, then looked at the last starfish of her last load and said as she threw it into the sea, "It makes a difference to this one!"

Sometimes, even small acts can make a big difference in the lives of others. Peter Copen, of The GLOBE Project, told me how some school children raised money to buy rope pumps for several villages in Nicaragua. The simple rope pump uses a bicycle wheel for a pulley and little cups that haul up water. Its use allows the top of a well to be covered, keeping the water clean and healthy.

The villagers were thrilled when they received the pumps, and the school children were thrilled, too, especially when they received a letter from a 10-year-old girl who said that because she no longer had to walk 12 kilometers to fetch clean water every morning, she was able to begin going to school.

Just as the shepherd had to wait many months to see if any of his tree seedlings grew, we may not see the results of our efforts immediately. It may also take time before other people recognize and give their support to any new idea. But whether others help or not, we should go ahead and do what we believe is right. Mother Teresa started her famous work with the poor by simply picking up and caring for one person who was dying on the streets of Calcutta. Her example of loving care for others has inspired thousands to do the same.

Date:

A Letter to Myself

During your visits you've had many chances to discover new things about nature and about yourself. You've witnessed many natural events, like the sunset and sunrise. Take a few minutes to write a letter to yourself and tell what you've learned. Here are some questions you might like to answer:

1. What things would I like to remember?

2. What would I like to tell others?

3. How can I continue to help my special place?

4. How have I changed?

5. What does "the Heart of Nature" mean to me?

Answering these questions will give you a record of the special moments you've had at your site. Save your letter, then after two weeks read it again. In that way you'll be able to remember what was really important to you.

By now, you've come to know many of the plants and animals that live at your site, and you've probably begun to feel a special friendship with them. Why not say good-bye to your nature-friends, as if you were leaving human friends. The following poem, titled *The Birds of the Air*, is one way to say farewell and to express your appreciation for the birds, trees, and all of nature in your area. I wrote this poem as a celebration of our oneness with nature.

The birds of the air are my brothers,
All flowers my sisters,
The trees are my friends.

All living creatures,
Mountains, and streams,
I take into my care.

For this green earth is our Mother,
Hidden in the sky is the Spirit above.

I share one Life with all who are here;
To everyone I give my love,

To everyone I give my love.

I've discovered that when I say this poem outdoors and express my love for nature with deep feeling, wild things often respond in kind. Many times I've noticed that flocks of birds have flown in and begun to sing all around me after I've spoken the words to *The Birds of the Air* poem with deep love.

To give thanks for all the special times you've had in nature, look off in a direction that you feel is especially beautiful, then say the lines of the poem directly to the birds, flowers, and hills that surround you. When you say "The trees are my friends," think of all the things you like about trees and send out thoughts of friendship and goodwill to the ones near you. As you say each line, think similar thoughts of appreciation. Repeat *The Birds of the Air* as many times as you wish.

Can you think of another way to express your appreciation? Maybe you'd like to read a poem you've written, or sing a song to say farewell in your own way.

Before you leave, take some time to clean up your campsite and return it to its natural condition. Then take a final walk and say good-bye to the plants, animals, and places you've come to know.

Your experience of *Journey to the Heart of Nature* can help others. If you write and tell us your discoveries and experiences, we'll share them with others.
Sharing Nature Foundation, 14618 Tyler Foote Road, Nevada City, California 95959 USA.

Saying Goodbye

Leader's Guide

The Role of the Leader

The adult mentor plays a key role in *Journey to the Heart of Nature*. Rachel Carson said, "If a child is to keep alive his inborn sense of wonder...he needs the companionship of at least one adult who can share it, rediscovering with him the joy, excitement, and mystery of the world we live in."

Your enthusiasm for nature will be your greatest asset. Therefore, don't be overly concerned if you lack training in the natural sciences. No one, no matter what his or her expertise, can answer *all* the questions generated by curious children. Your excitement and desire to help young people find their own answers is what will make *Journey to the Heart of Nature* a success.

Although each young person chooses his or her own specific site, you should try to select the best general area you can for the visits. A place with interesting terrain and a variety of habitats will help to awaken a sense of adventure and curiosity. Taking the time to locate such an area is well worth the extra effort.

The stories in the book create a keen interest in the activities. To keep the stories fresh and motivational, it's best to save them until the young person is about to go to the special place. As the leader, however, you'll want to read through the book beforehand to become familiar with the visits and to introduce the program effectively.

Since there are many activities to choose from, you should feel free to emphasize those activities you feel will work best for you, and stay with them as long as interest is high. The overall enthusiasm for nature is much more important than what can be learned from any one activity.

Safety Concerns

As the responsible adult, you'll need to decide whether a young person can be left alone without supervision. Level of maturity, outdoor experience, and the presence of other people in the area should be considered, as well as any potential physical dangers. Avoid, for example, cliffs and avalanche zones, and areas where quicksand or flash floods might occur. You should also determine if dangerous animals are a threat. If you are unfamiliar with the region, contact someone who can tell you the important information you should know.

Before a young person visits the site for the first time, inform him or her of any poisonous plants or animals and other possible hazards such as lightning or impure water. On Visit Five, you may want to camp with or near the young person, or plan late evening and early morning visits if an overnight stay isn't advisable.

Planning for Special Uses

Regular Program

Journey to the Heart of Nature works equally well in camp settings or on field trips. At a camp, for example, you could plan a visit each day, while with a youth group or class, field trips could be scheduled once a week for five weeks. Each visit has a particular theme.

Visit One: The reader chooses and begins to explore a special place in nature.

Visit Two: Suggests ways to become familiar with animals and plants that live in the area.

Visit Three: Encourages receptivity to nature.

Visit Four: Suggests ways to preserve and care for the site and to share its special features with a friend.

Visit Five: Encourages personal reflection during an evening/morning or overnight visit to the site.

Visits One, Two, and Three take about an hour and a half of field time. The time required for Visit Four depends on the conservation project you select plus about 30 minutes for the *Sharing with a Friend* section. If the young person will not be staying overnight on Visit Five, allow two and a half hours for the evening and one hour for the morning.

Because of the need for writing, try to avoid wet weather visits. Reasonably comfortable weather also makes for longer, more enjoyable periods of quiet observation. In some areas you may want to time your visits to avoid natural inconveniences, such as afternoon thunderstorms or mosquitoes which are usually active at dawn and dusk.

Feel free to combine, extract, and rearrange the activities from the various visits to fit your needs. The following sections give suggestions for weekends and single visits.

Weekend Use

If you want to complete the program in a weekend, you could follow a schedule like this:

Friday late afternoon—Visit One

Friday night—group meeting

Saturday morning—activities from Visits Two & Three

Saturday afternoon—conservation project from Visit Four

Saturday evening/Sunday early morning—Visit Five

Sunday mid-morning—*Sharing Your Site with a Friend*, Visit Four

Single Visit Experience

If you are visiting a natural area only once, here are some suggested activities you might choose from:

Awakening Enthusiasm

An excellent way to encourage enthusiasm for *Journey to the Heart of Nature* is a group gathering. You might want to introduce the program at a first meeting, then get together after each visit to share experiences and play nature activities with the group. A breakfast get-together after the overnight visit can be especially meaningful.

If the group members visit their individual areas at the same time, you may need to plan extra activities or stories for those who finish early. (For additional ideas and games, see *Sharing Nature with Children* and *Sharing the Joy of Nature*, available from Dawn Publications.)

Try to think of creative ways to introduce the activities. For example, before the group members go out to find their special spots, you can show them a map of the area that is labeled with exciting names such as Giant of the Woods, Inland Sea, Unexplored Territory, Troll's Bathtub, and Cathedral Forest.

Another effective way to encourage exploration and observation is to take photographs of interesting features and views in the area and ask the group to try to find the site of each picture.

Introductory Field Experience

Another good way to create interest is to lead the group through some of the activities before you introduce the complete program. After they've had fun doing the activities together, young people are much more likely to apply themselves enthusiastically on their own.

The following recommended activities take a little over an hour to play. Keep the group in the same general area, then gather them after each activity for discussion and directions.

Activity	Page	Time Required*
The Adventure Hunt	(22)	*15 minutes*
Meet a Tree	(85)	*15 minutes*
The Poetry of Your Site	(58)	*20 minutes*
Uplifting Story	(select)	*5 minutes*

Times do not include sharing time.

When using the *Adventure Hunt* with a group, send the players out individually, then call everyone back as soon as some have finished, and divide them into groups of four so they can share their discoveries. (Small groups encourage more involvement than a single large group.) After five minutes or so of sharing, have everyone point in the direction of their best view. There's always much laughter when the children extend their arms pointing in all directions.

To play *Meet a Tree* with a large group, you'll need to find a wooded area with trees of different species, sizes and shapes. (Check also to make sure the forest floor is relatively free of undergrowth and that there are no poisonous plants or other hazards.)

Children who aren't old enough to guide a partner safely can pair up with an adult or older child. When introducing *Meet a Tree*, it's especially important to tell young guides to be gentle and careful while leading their blindfolded companion.

For *The Poetry of Your Site* activity, you may want to make a group Vertical Poem first, before sending everyone out to do their own. Afterwards, meet all-together or in small groups.

My Special Spot: A Group Activity

My Special Spot gives everyone a chance to be alone in nature while in a group. This activity is ideal in situations where the children are too young to be left unsupervised; when there's not enough time for a regular visit; or as a quick introduction. Before using this activity, it's best to play a few active, group-oriented nature activities like the ones mentioned in *Sharing Nature with Children* and *Sharing the Joy of Nature*.

Give each player a pencil and a *My Special Spot* activity sheet. Tell them that they must each find their own special place in nature. Once they've found their spots, the players will choose from the activities from the list that most interest them. (If you would like more information on the Vertical Poem, (#6 next page), refer to *The Poetry of Your Site* activity on page 58. For *Bird Calling*, (#3 next page), you'll want to substitute a different bird calling sound if you are somewhere other than North America or Europe.) Designate the area where everyone is to search for a spot, and make arrangements for everyone to return at the same time (use a watch or a loud sound).

Once everyone has finished, have each person make an invitation from an index card. (See sample drawing below.) Ask half of the group to put their cards into a hat, then have those with cards left over draw a card out of the hat. Once they've picked a card, they should pair up with the person whose card they've drawn. Then, for example, if Mary picks Barbara's card, Mary keeps Barbara's card and gives her own to Barbara. Then Barbara and Mary go off to share their special spots with each other. Have the pairs share the activities they've done, as well as anything else they've discovered about their special spots.

Write your name and your special spot's name in the invitation card below:

You are Invited to Explore:

_____

Your Guide is:

_____

My Special Spot Activity Sheet

1) *Think of a name* for your special spot:

2) *The Best View:* Find your best view and make a sketch of it. Later, you'll share the sketch with a friend. (See if he or she can find it.)

3) *Bird Calling:* If you hear small birds, stand or sit very still near some bushes or trees, and repeat the *"pssh"* sound several times in sets of four: *"pssh...pssh...pssh...pssh."* Repeat the four-part call three to five times, then pause to listen. Continue *"psshing"* and listening. The birds will respond in a few minutes or not at all. Write down what happened, and describe the birds you saw.

4) *Sounds:* Find the best place to listen for nature sounds. Then, see if you can hear at least four different sounds in less than a minute. (If the area is quiet, you can take longer.) See if you can figure out what is making the sounds. Write down the sounds:

1)_____

2)_____

3)_____

4)_____

*)_____

*)_____

5) *Letting Others Know:* Which part of your spot is most special to you? In the space below, describe what it is. Later, you'll give your description to a friend, and ask him or her to find it.

6) *Vertical Poem:* Choose a word that captures the feeling of the place you've chosen. Write each letter of the word in the column at the left. Then use each letter to begin a line of your poem.

____ _____

____ _____

____ _____

____ _____

____ _____

____ _____

____ _____

The Fifth Visit: Special Considerations

Sunset Watch

After setting up camp and going for a walk around the site, try to arrive at your watch spot about 15 minutes before actual sundown for this activity. Because you'll be sitting for at least another 30 minutes after sundown, a long wait beforehand might make a young person restless. You may want to bring a star chart along to identify the constellations.

Campfires

I didn't recommend making a campfire in Visit Five for the following reasons: the purpose of Visit Five is to encourage experiencing the world at night, and a campfire's light reduces one's ability to see; it's risky for inexperienced campers to build fires unsupervised; and a campfire can negatively impact the environment in the area.

In some places and at certain times of the year, a campfire may be appropriate. (Young campers in particular will find a fire comforting and companionable.) If you decide that your campers are sufficiently skilled in safe fire-building practices, you might compromise by suggesting that they have a *small* campfire after completing the star-viewing activities. (It's best to use an existing fire ring, if one is available.)

Before giving the group permission to build a fire, you will of course need to find out if it's legal to build fires, and if there are regulations for where and how fires should be built. Make sure everyone who wants to build a fire has had training on how to build fires safely. Good sources of information on building fires are the *Boy Scouts of America Handbook* and *Fieldbook*. (See page 118 for some guidelines from these books.) You'll also want to contact the local forestry or park agency for information.

In a large group of solo campers, you should consider prohibiting campfires in order to reduce the impact on the area.

Human Waste

Whether a young person stays overnight or not, every visitor needs to be taught how to properly dispose of human waste, preferably before Visit One. See page 118 for more information.

Follow-up after the Journey

Ongoing Care For The Site

After completing the visits, many young people will have established a real bond with their special place. If they live nearby, they can continue to develop this relationship with the help of other activities. Books such as *The Earth Manual*, which was referred to in Visit Four, suggest a variety of ways to become involved in the long-term care of the site.

New Journeys

During the five visits, a young person may express special interest in a particular aspect of nature, such as rocks or trees. This is a golden opportunity to introduce him or her to a resource person who can further encourage this interest. Many individuals and nature organizations will be eager to share their knowledge.

The Birds of the Air

Groups enjoy singing *The Birds of the Air* and using its Indian sign language-like movements. These hand and arm motions express in a beautiful way the meaning of the words. Using these movements while singing the lines makes a wonderful closing activity.

The birds of the air are my brothers,
Stretch both arms out to the side, turning the palms down. Gracefully wave the arms as if they were bird wings.

All flowers my sisters,
Bring the palms together in front of you, then spread your fingers apart like the opening of a flower.

The trees are my friends,
Join the palms together above your head and sway your body like the trunk of a tree.

All living creatures,
Bring your hands down to your heart, then sweep both arms out to the front and to the sides in welcome to all creatures.

Mountains,
Bring your fingertips together at chin level to form a mountain peak.

And streams,

Keeping your left hand at the chin, sweep your right arm out to the side fluttering the fingers like rippling water.

I take unto my care.

Cup one hand on top of the other, palms up at heart level, holding all nature in your care.

For this green earth is our Mother,

Sweep your hands up and out from the heart, reaching out to include the whole earth.

Hidden in the sky is the Spirit above.

Look upward, extending your arms toward the sky.

I share one Life with all who are here;

Cross your hands at the heart.

To everyone I give my love,

Keeping the right hand at your heart, sweep the left hand out to the side with the palm up.

To everyone I give my love.

Keeping the left hand out to the side, sweep the right hand out to the other side, again with palm up.

Sheet music for *The Birds of the Air* can be found in my book *Sharing the Joy of Nature*. The song can be heard on the nature games audio cassette, *A Day in the Forest*. The arm and hand movements are demonstrated on the *Sharing the Joy of Nature Video*. All are available from Dawn Publications.

Resources for the Leader

The books in the following list are all excellent resources for stories, outdoor living skills, and natural history. The first three books are of special interest to young people, while the remaining books are directed more to the group leader. When a title isn't self-explanatory, a short description is included. Ask a local naturalist, librarian, or bookstore clerk to recommend field guides specific to your area.

My Side of the Mountain, by Jean George. Copyright 1959. Scholastic Book Services, New York, New York. A boy's year-long adventure living alone in the wilderness. (Fiction)

Julie of the Wolves, by Jean George. Copyright 1972. Harper Collins Publishers, New York, New York. A young Inuit girl, lost in the Alaska wilderness, survives by being accepted by a pack of Arctic wolves. (Fiction)

The Tracker, by Tom Brown Jr. Copyright 1978. Berkley Books, New York, New York. Tom Brown's true-life apprenticeship as a young boy to an Apache Indian tracker, Stalking Wolf. The lessons Tom Brown learned include how to wait, how to listen, and how to see. (Non-Fiction)

Boy Scouts of America Handbook and *Fieldbook*. Copyright 1990 & 1984. Boy Scouts of America, Irving, Texas. Two excellent sources for campfire building skills and wilderness safety, as well as many other outdoor living topics.

Tom Brown's Field Guide to Nature and Survival for Children, by Tom Brown Jr. Copyright 1989. Berkley Books, New York. Good information on tracking, camping, wildlife observation, and outdoor safety.

The Earth Manual, by Malcolm Margolin. Copyright 1975. Heyday Books, Berkeley, California. An informative, easy-to-read book about caring for the land, with many conservation projects.

The Way Nature Works. Copyright 1992. Macmillan Publishing Co., New York, New York. An illustrated resource for understanding the natural world.

Peterson First Guide to Astronomy, by Jay M. Pasachoff. Copyright 1988. Houghton Mifflin Company, Boston, Massachusetts.

Field Guide to the Birds of North America. Copyright 1983. National Geographic Society, Washington, D.C.

Field Guide to the Mammals, Peterson Field Guide Series, by William H. Burt. Copyright 1964. Houghton Mifflin Co., Boston, Massachusetts.

Pond Life, by George K. Reid and Herbert S. Zim. Copyright 1967. Golden Press, New York, New York. Easy to read and use.

Sierra Club Naturalist's Guide Series, Sierra Club, San Francisco, California. Informative regional field guides.

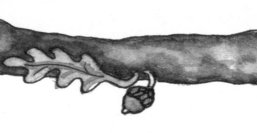

Keepers of the Earth, *Keepers of the Animals*, and *Keepers of the Night*, by Michael J. Caduto and Joseph Bruchac. Copyright 1988, 1991, & 1994. Fulcrum Publishing, Golden, Colorado. Native American stories, natural history information and activities for children ages 5 through 12.

Guidelines for Campfire Safety and Disposal of Human Waste

(Excerpted from the *Boy Scout of America Handbook* and *Fieldbook*)

Human Wastes

Disposing of human waste outdoors requires special care. If you are by yourself or with a small group, dig a cathole.

Find a secluded spot at least 200 feet (75 steps or more) from water, campsites, and trails. Use your heel or a camp shovel to dig a shallow hole no more than 6 inches deep. Organisms in the top layers of earth will break down human waste and small amounts of toilet paper. After you have used the cathole, fill it with soil and replace any ground cover.

Bury nothing in a cathole except human waste. Animals will dig up buried garbage and scatter it around. Materials such as plastic, glass, metal, and cardboard may take many years to decompose. Take all your trash home with you. "If you packed it in, you can pack it out."

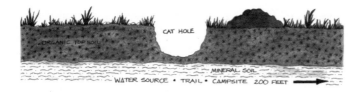

Campfires

From the moment you light a fire until it is completely out, it is your responsibility to keep it under control.

Making a Safe Fire Site

If the ground cover is fragile, or if the forest is dry, or if the wind is strong, or if wood is scarce, or if there is a chance of creating a new scar on the land, responsible campers forego open fires.

However, when conditions are safe, and proper permits have been obtained, group members can make a fire just big enough for their needs, then dismantle it so that not the slightest clue remains that the fire site ever existed.

A safe fire site is one on which nothing will burn except the fuel you use to feed the fire. It's also a spot from which flames cannot spread.

Choose a spot on gravel, sand, or bare soil, well away from trees and bushes, dry grasses, and anything else that might burn. Look overhead for branches that sparks could ignite. Stay clear of boulders that may be blackened by smoke, or large tree roots that might be harmed by too much heat.

Clean the fire site down to bare soil, then remove all burnable material from the ground around it. The cleared circle should be 10 feet or more across. Rake away pine needles, leaves, twigs, and anything else that could catch fire from a flying ember. Save the ground cover so that you can replace it when you are done with your fire. Keep a pot of water close to the fire site for emergencies.

If the site is grassy, use your camp shovel to cut around and under a two-foot-wide square of sod. Lift out the loosened sod, lay it right side up in the shade, and sprinkle it with water. The grass should stay fresh until you replace it as you break camp.

Archaeologists uncovering the remains of ancient civilizations find rocks still smudged by fires that burned thousands of years ago. Before building a fire on bare rock, put down a two-inch layer of sand or soil; otherwise, your fire may leave a permanent black stain. If you scatter the protective layer when you are done, the stone should be unmarked.

Putting out a Fire

Extinguish every fire when it is no longer needed. Make sure it is *COLD OUT*, not just out. That means the ashes are so cool you can touch any part of the fire with your hands.

With water: Splash water on the embers. Stir the damp ashes with a stick and splash them again. Turn smoldering sticks and wet them on all sides. Use plenty of water. Repeat until you can touch every part of the fire.

Without water: When water is scarce, work sand or dirt into the coals. Keep stirring soil through the fire until it is out. Rub burned sticks against the ground to extinguish embers. Give the fire the *COLD OUT* test by touching the dirt and dead ashes with your hands.

Cleaning a Fire Ring

After extinguishing a fire in an old fire ring, pick out all bits of paper, foil, and unburned food, and pack them home in a trash bag. Bury the ashes. Leave the fire ring clean for other campers.

Erasing a Fire Ring

If you've made a new fire ring, it's best to take it apart and erase all evidence of your fire. Scatter any rocks, turning their blackened sides to the ground. Bury cold ashes and replace ground cover and sod, and toss away extra firewood. When you're done, the site should look just as it did when you found it.

Listing of Quotations & Stories

Guidelines:

Page 8: Turn them loose..." John Burroughs

Visit One

Page 11: "Walk away quietly ..." John Muir, *The Wilderness World of John Muir*, edited by Edwin Way Teale, page 311. Copyright 1954. Houghton Mifflin Co., Boston, Massachusetts.
Page 14: Pine marten
Page 18: "wandering through the jungles..." Jim Corbett. *Man-Eaters of Kumaon*, page xvii. Copyright 1946. Oxford University Press, New York, New York.
Page 24: Claude Monet
Page 25: "For observing nature, the best pace..." Edwin Way Teale
Page 26: George Washington Carver

Visit Two

Page 30: Orchard Birds
Page 32: Tom Brown Jr. and Stalking Wolf
Page 37: "Pelorus Jack," by Cyrus Cress, found in *The Audubon Book of True Nature Stories*, selected and edited by John K. Terres, pages 113-118. Copyright 1958. Thomas Y. Crowell Company, New York, New York.
Page 38: "let me name all the new birds..." Ohiyesa (Charles E. Eastman), *Indian Boyhood*,

pages 52-53. Copyright 1902. University of Nebraska Press, Lincoln, Nebraska.
Page 42: "When we try to pick out anything..." John Muir, *Son of the Wilderness: The Life of John Muir*, by Linnie Marsh Wolfe, pages 123-124. Copyright 1973, University of Wisconsin Press, Madison, Wisconsin.

Visit Three

Page 46: Story of Godo Nakanishi, thanks to Hiraku Haga
Page 48: Family of beaver
Page 48: "the clearing became alive with monkeys..." J. Allen Boone, *The Language of Silence*, page 70. Copyright 1970. Harper & Row Publishers, New York, New York.
Page 53: Fable of the two dogs
Page 53: "This world is so beautiful..." Ralph Waldo Emerson
Page 53: "With beauty before me ..." from *American Indian Poetry,* edited by George W. Cronyn. Liveright/W.W. Norton Co., New York, New York.
Page 56: The story of the wise man is based on similar stories in the *Srimad Bhagavatum.*
Page 57: "We always have considered our wild animals ..." The Dalai Lama of Tibet, *My Tibet*, page 61. Copyright 1990. University of California Press, Berkeley, California.
Pages 58-59: Haiku poems by Basho and Buson, *Haiku Harvest* and *Cherry Blossoms*. Peter Pauper Press, White Plains, New York.

Visit Four

Pages 61-63: Story of Stickeen, John Muir, *Stickeen*, pages 33, 48, 53-54, 57, 61, 63-64, 68-70. Copyright 1909. Heyday Books, Berkeley, California.
Page 65: "Did you know trees talk?" Walking Buffalo, *Touch the Earth*, compiled by T.C. McLuhan, page 23. Copyright 1971. Simon & Schuster, New York.
Page 65: "enlarged my life, extended its boundaries." John Muir, *John of the Mountains: The Unpublished Journals of John Muir*, edited by Linnie Marsh Wolfe, page 277. Copyright 1938. University of Wisconsin Press, Madison, Wisconsin.
Page 65: Zoo gorilla

Page 68: "If you love it enough..." George Washington Carver

Page 69: "Human and animal love..." John Muir, *John of the Mountains: The Unpublished Journals of John Muir*, edited by Linnie Marsh Wolfe, page 277. Copyright 1938. University of Wisconsin Press, Madison, Wisconsin.

Pages 72-73: "One day I was playing in the mud of a rice field..." Paul Brand, *A Handful of Mud: A Personal History of My Love for the Soil*, found in *Tending the Garden*, edited by Wesley Granberg-Michaelson. Copyright 1987. William B. Eerdmans Publishing Co., Grand Rapids, Michigan.

Page 81: "'The Giving Tree': Alison and the Sugar Pine," condensed from Chris Bowman's article in *The Sacramento Bee*, May 11, 1993, page 1. Copyright 1993.

Page 82: Story of John Muir and Teddy Roosevelt from *Son of the Wilderness: A Life of John Muir*, by Linnie Marsh Wolfe, pages 289-293. Copyright 1945 by Alfred A. Knopf. Inc., New York, New York.

Visit Five

Page 91: "[Nature] is never the same..." Clarence Dutton, *Tertiary History of the Grand Canyon District*, published in 1882.

Page 96: "When alone at night..." John Muir, *John of the Mountains: The Unpublished Journals of John Muir*, edited by Linnie Marsh Wolfe, page 295. Copyright 1938. University of Wisconsin Press, Madison, Wisconsin.

Page 98: "To enable my 8 camels ..." Sir Francis Younghusband, *The Heart of Nature*, pages 116-118. Copyright 1921. John Murray, London, England.

Page 99: "After arrival in camp ..." Sir Francis Younghusband, *The Heart of Nature*, pages 167 & 168.

Page 101: "The time to hear bird music..." Donald Culross Peattie

Pages 105-106: A retelling of *The Man Who Planted Hope and Grew Happiness* by Jean Giono. Thanks to Friends of Nature, Brooksville, Maine, 1967.

Page 107: Woman and starfish

Page 107: Value of rope pumps in a village in Nicaragua

Page 110: "The Birds of the Air," Joseph Cornell, *Listening to Nature*, page 25. Copyright 1987. Dawn Publications, Nevada City, California.

Leader's Guide

Page 112: "If a child is to keep alive..." Rachel Carson, *The Sense of Wonder*, page 45. Copyright 1956. Harper & Row Publishers, New York, New York.

Pages 118-119: Campfire safety and human waste disposal, *Boy Scouts of America Handbook* pages 50, 82, 83, and 93, and *Fieldbook*, pages 100, 101, and 111. Copyrights 1990 and 1984. Boy Scouts of America, Irving, Texas.

ACKNOWLEDGMENTS

First and foremost, I would like to acknowledge Michael Deranja's invaluable contributions to *Journey to the Heart of Nature*. Michael originally suggested a series of visits to a special place in nature, and we subsequently enjoyed many brainstorming sessions during which he put together the first working prototype of the book. Michael's special gift is clear thinking, and much of the book's clear format reflects his loving labors. Working with Michael was a joy.

The World Scout Bureau proposed the idea of a book for young people, and I want to express my gratitude to this fine organization for their help and encouragement. I am especially grateful to Jacques Moreillon, Malek Gabr, Jim Sharp, Dan Hinckley, Philippe Pijollet, and Dr. Adolfo Aristeguieta Gramcko. Special thanks also to Klaus Jacobs and the Johann Jacobs Foundation, whose generous and enthusiastic support of the *Scouting for Nature and Environment* program made this book possible.

I am especially grateful also to Hiraku Haga of Kashiwa Shobo Publishing Co. for researching the life of Godo Nakanishi from many sources; to Bruce and Carol Malnor for letting me know about Vertical Poems; and to Masahito Yoshida of Nature Games (Japan) for sharing his Interview with Nature activity.

Writing a book for young people all over the world was a challenge. It was made easier by the many valuable suggestions I received from the following people who critically read the manuscript and offered comments and suggestions: Dr. Jay Casbon, Lewis & Clark College; Kurt Cunningham, Montana Dept. of Fish & Wildlife; Susan Dermond; Pete Devine, Yosemite Institute; Bruce Forman, California Dept. of Fish & Game; Steve Gilzow; Peter Goering; Tim Henke, Fairfield Osborne Nature Conservancy Preserve; Ralph Ingleton, Forest Valley Outdoor Ed. Centre, Canada; Carolyn Kennedy and Donna Nye from the national office of the Girl Scouts of the USA; Vance Martin, International Wilderness Leadership Foundation; Tom Mullin, Fairfax County Park Authority; Duane Rhodes and Don Cornell from the Boy Scouts of America's Columbia Pacific Council; Kenneth Rich; Dr. Rocky Rohwedder, California State University at Sonoma; Klas Sandell, University of Orebro, Sweden; Craig Sarbeck, Educo International; Cathy Setterlin, The Pratt Nature Center; Roy Simpson, Chiricahua National Monument; David Tribe, Manly Vale Public School and The Gould League, Australia; and my many friends at the Education for Life Foundation.

Finally, I would like to thank my wife for her insight, support and friendship. Knowing my work so well, Anandi made a significant contribution to *Journey to the Heart of Nature*.

About Joseph Cornell

Joseph Cornell grew up exploring the marshes, rivers, and mountains near his home town of Yuba City in northern California. Joseph designed his own bachelor's degree program in Nature Awareness at California State University in Chico. He received his formal training as a naturalist from the National Audubon Society, and spent seven years teaching in public school outdoor education programs and as a naturalist with the Boy Scouts of America.

Soon after the publication of his first book, *Sharing Nature with Children*, Cornell founded Sharing Nature Foundation, an organization through which he shares his methods and philosophy with adult leaders and teachers. His workshops on nature awareness have been attended by many thousands of people around the world. *Sharing Nature with Children* has become a classic in the nature education field, and has sold over 350,000 copies. Foreign editions have been published in Japan, the Netherlands, Germany, Spain, Yugoslavia, Greece, Italy, Great Britain, Central African Republic, Taiwan, Denmark, Latvia, and France. Other popular books by Mr. Cornell are *Sharing the Joy of Nature* and *Listening to Nature*.

Joseph and his wife have lived for many years at Ananda World Brotherhood Village, one of the most successful intentional communities in the world.

About Michael Deranja

Michael Deranja has a Master's Degree in Education from the University of California at Berkeley and is the founder of the Ananda School. Michael drew on his background in education to help in developing the structure of *Journey to the Heart of Nature*.

Long-time friends, Joseph and Michael have collaborated on a number of projects in the field of education.

Joseph Cornell and teachers he has personally trained offer nature-awareness workshops throughout the year. The programs are based on Joseph's years of experience teaching nature awareness. They draw extensively on activities and philosophy from *Sharing Nature with Children, Sharing the Joy of Nature, Listening to Nature,* and *Journey to the Heart of Nature.*

Mr. Cornell leads a yearly summer retreat called *Sharing the Joy of Nature.* Participants experience many ways of deepening their enjoyment of the natural world and come away with effective and inspirational tools they can use whenever they go out in nature.

To learn more about *Journey to the Heart of Nature* and other programs for personal and professional inspiration, call or write: Sharing Nature Foundation, 14618 Tyler Foote Road, Nevada City, California 95959. Phone (916) 292-3893.

Education for Life Foundation

Sharing Nature Foundation is affiliated with the Education for Life Foundation, which offers books, tapes, workshops, and seminars on holistic, transformational education. *Journey to the Heart of Nature* is one aspect of the Education for Life curriculum, which addresses children's total educational needs: heart, body, spirit and mind. Michael Deranja is the founder of the Ananda School, the original school where the Education for Life philosophy has been developed and applied. For information, write or call: Education for Life Foundation, 14618 Tyler Foote Road, Nevada City, California 95959. Phone (916) 292-3775.

CREDITS

Book Design: Sara Cryer and Josh Gitomer
Cover Design: Sara Cryer
Production: Robert Froelick
Illustrations:

Elizabeth Ann Kelley: 4, 28, 35, 36/37, 41, 46/47, 49, 51, 52, 59, 64, 76/77, 98/99,
Helen Strang: 18, 22, 43, 44/45, 50, 55, 56/57, 70/71, 72/73, 86/87, 104, 110/111
Karen White: 7, 9, 14, 15, 16/17, 20, 25, 30, 31, 32, 33, 34, 54, 60/61, 62/63, 66, 74, 80,
    84, 89, 92, 94/95, 96, 100/101, 102, 103, 108, 124
Nalini Snell: 30, 67
Sara Moffat: 12
Illustrator Unknown: 38/39

Photography:

John Hendrickson: Front Cover
Rodney Polden: 90
Shmuel Thaler: 13, 19
Steven Thomas: 11
Wayne Green: Back Cover, 2/3, 10, 26/27, 68/69, 91
Yosemite National Trust: 83

Other books by Joseph Cornell

Sharing Nature With Children $7.95

An internationally recognized classic, *Sharing Nature with Children* helps children become more aware of the world around them and gives them the deep personal satisfaction of being in touch with the earth. Cornell has mastered a playful approach to learning the delights of nature. This book is perfect for parents, teachers, youth groups, and church groups. Suitable for children of all ages.

"Absolutely the best awareness-of-nature book I've ever seen. It works for adults too."
— *Whole Earth Catalog*

Listening to Nature $12.95

A lavishly photographed nature awareness guidebook for adults. This practical handbook will show you how to enter the quiet mystery of the natural world. Rediscover your connection with nature through this unique combination of Cornell's ever-popular nature awareness activities, inspiring quotes from the likes of Muir and Throeau, and 41 stunning color photographs by Sierra Club Calendar veteran John Hendrickson.

*"**Listening to Nature** is a gentle and powerful gift. Read it, live it, and then, as Joseph Cornell quotes John Muir, — 'Nature's peace will flow into you as sunshine flows into trees.' "*
— *Cheryl Charles, Director, Project Wild*

Sharing the Joy of Nature $9.95

Joseph's second book completes the process begun with *Sharing Nature with Children.* Through introducing his remarkable technique of Flow Learning, Joseph shows how to match activities to the interest and energy levels of children, thus ensuring a successful nature experience. By applying these principles, parents and teachers will discover that you don't need to be a naturalist in order to awaken children's enthusiasm for the outdoors. Learn Build-A-Tree, Sound Map, and 18 other new activities.

*"**Sharing the Joy of Nature** flows so naturally from **Sharing Nature With Children** that the two should become companion volumes in every naturalist's library."* — *Vincent Kehoe, Executive Director, Yosemite Institute*

Audio and Video

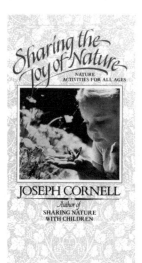

Sharing the Joy of Nature Video $22.95

Watch Joseph Cornell in action with a group of children and adults in the high country of the Sierra Nevada mountains. In this 40-minute video you will see how easy it is to lead fun, educational, cooperative nature awareness games using *Flow Learning*. See how this technique matches various types of activities to the children's changing levels of interest and energy. 8 delightful games from his book of the same name.

"A gorgeous video! Very useful for teachers and anyone else who works with children and nature."
— *Children's Video Report*

Listening to Nature Audio Cassette $10.98

A serene audio journey to a variety of natural settings including a visit to the seashore, an interlude at a wilderness lake, and quiet time by a mountain stream. The 60 minutes of soothing natural sounds are interspersed with recitations of 12 of the most inspiring quotations from the book, *Listening to Nature*. Older teens to adults.

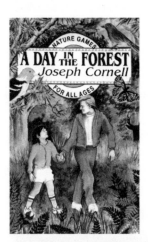

A Day in the Forest $9.95
Audio Cassette

Let's go for a walk in the forest and meet a lot of interesting creatures along the way. Guess and draw the mystery animal, imagine how a tree feels during the four seasons, sing the *Song of the Three-Toed Sloth* or learn to call different birds. Games and activities for children ages 7-12. Additional adult resources on side two. 75 minutes.

Boundless Forever:
A Musical Tribute to the Wilderness $9.95

This 60-minute audio cassette presents a unique collection of songs that celebrate the beauty and inspiration gained from natural areas around the world. The musical arrangements provide a broad range of vocal harmonies and instrumentation against a background of natural sounds that include icebergs, the desert wind, seagulls, and the tropical rainforest.

"Filled with enchanting sounds of flute, piano, and harp, ... a great present for your favorite green teenager."
— *New Age Retailer*

Other Nature Products

Animal Clue $7.50

A set of 2 decks of question and answer cards introduces 17 different indoor and outdoor games for children aged 7-13. Topics explored include: animal empathy, wildlife observation skills, the balance of nature, and predator/prey relationships. Parents and teachers, scout and youth group leaders around the country have found that the games foster cooperation, friendly competition, and creative expression. Some games can be played by two children, others by up to 40 or more. Children ages 8-13.

Nature Meditations $3.50

Each of the 20 cards in this popular two-color deck offers an inspirational quotation from people such as Walt Whitman, Helen Keller, and Native Americans, and an activity to enhance its meaning. Great for backpacking trips or a walk through a city park. Older teens to adults.